LONDON'S
EAST END
TRACTION
Steam, Diesel & Electric

Copyright Book Law Publications – First published in the United Kingdom in 2019
ISBN 978-1-909625-99-0
Printed and bound by The Amadeus Press, Cleckheaton, West Yorkshire
Published by Book Law Publications, 382 Carlton Hill, Nottingham, NG4 1JA

LONDON'S EAST END TRACTION

By D. Brennand

ABBREVIATIONS USED THROUGHOUT THIS BOOK

AEI	Associated Electrical Industries
BR	British Railways
BRCW	Birmingham Railway Carriage & Wagon Co.
BTH	British Thompson-Houston
DLR	Docklands Light Railway
DMU	Diesel Multiple Unit
DRS	Diesel Repair Shop
ECML	East Coast Main Line
EE	English Electric Company
EMU	Electric Multiple Unit
ETH	Electric Train Heating
EWS	English Welsh & Scottish Railways
GER	Great Eastern Railway
GN	Great Northern
GW	Great Western
HST	High Speed Train
LCGB	Locomotive Club of Great Britain
LEER	London's East End Railways
LMS	London Midland & Scottish Railway
LNER	London & North Eastern Railway
LNWR	London & North Western Railway
LT&SR	London Tilbury & Southend Railway
MET CAM	Metropolitan-Cammell
NBL	North British Locomotive Company
NLR	North London Railway
NRM	National Railway Museum
OHL	Overhead Line (Power Supply)
PLA	Port of London Authority
RCTS	Railway Correspondence & Travel Society
SIFT	London (Stratford) International Freight Terminal
SR	Southern Railway/Region
T&FGJR	Tottenham & Forest Gate Junction Railway
TOPS	Total Operations Processing System
WCML	West Coast Main Line

Dedicated to my wife Belinda. Hugely talented, kind and generous.
Only your unending support and encouragement over many years,
has made the London's East End series possible.

ACKNOWLEDGEMENTS

I would like to express my gratitude to the following people who have given me an enormous amount of help; Andy Meeks, Andy Grimmett, Dave Cockle, Jim Connor, Barry Dann, Roland Hummerston, Roger Jocelyn, Peter Kay, Peter Manley, Andrew Proctor, Graham Weller, Dave Underwood, Brian Pask, Geoff Silcock, Doug Fairhurst and of course, my wife Belinda who meticulously proof reads all my waffle. Also, the staff at Amadeus Press for their guidance and patience. If I have missed anybody, it was not intentional.

FRONT COVER: Very few images that I've ever seen portray the East End Traction theme better than this one taken in the summer of 1959 at Liverpool Street from the Taxi Rank. The past generation of steam sits blissfully unaware of its Nemesis in the shape of a very clean, virtually brand-new Brush Type 2 A1A-A1A 1470 H.P. No. D5530 (31112) new to March (31B) shed in May 1959. The N7 0-6-2T No. 69696 (LNER 2656) sits in the engine dock between platforms 12 and 13. It was reallocated from Stratford (30A) to Hatfield (34C) in October 1959 which helps to date the picture. Built by the William Beardmore Company in 1927, it spent two spells at Stratford, which became its final shed and graveyard in April 1961. In the background are three Class AM6 (306) 1949 Shenfield stock EMUs and two AM7 (307) 1956 Southend line EMUs in all over green livery. The eagle-eyed amongst you will recognise this picture from London's East End Diesels, but it has been reworked and given a rare second outing as I try very hard to only use rare or previously unpublished views. *(Author's Collection)*

BACK COVER TOP: This is the nearest thing to travelling back in time that we can have and in rare glorious colour. This was one of many railtours organised by the Locomotive Club of Great Britain (visit www.lcgb.org.uk) in the 1950s as our railway network was slowly shrinking. Beeching had not been heard of in railway circles, but rapid change and dieselisation was looming. This is the "Poplar & Edgware Tour" of 5th May 1956. The NLR 0-6-0T tank No. 58859 had worked the special from Broad Street and is seen at Millwall Junction. To the right is LMS 0-6-0T 3F Jinty No. 47484 waiting to work the train on the next leg to East Ham, Woodgrange Park and Stratford. To the right is Millwall Junction station (closed in 1926) and the signal box. To the left is Harrow Lane sidings and Blackwall Bridge signal box. *(Steam & Sail)*

BACK COVER BOTTOM: The Stratford drivers and fireman tasked with keeping the London Pilot clean have clearly not failed in their duties, as this lovely image of D8234 at Liverpool Street on 5th April 1964 testifies. Right from the end of steam in September 1962 until the withdrawal of the class in 1971, D8234 was chosen by Stratford to be the regular London Pilot engine. This view was taken on the West Side of the station and it is interesting to note that the short engine spurs left over from the steam era are still in situ, but the rusty rails prove that their time is limited. *(J. Boyes/Book Law)*

TITLE PAGE: This superb image of BR 'Britannia' class 7P6F 4-6-2 No. 70010 "Owen Glendower" heading east with a Liverpool Street to Norwich express through Bethnal Green on 7th September 1961 sums up our hobby and fascination with railways. The powerful locomotive has effortlessly surmounted Bethnal Green bank and the driver hangs out of the cab looking for that all-important green signal before he opens the regulator wide. The stirring sight and sound is witnessed by a couple of very lucky trainspotters on an old Great Eastern Railway bench. These are not kids, but grown men, wrapped up in the dark art that many of us would have followed in our formative years. The notebooks and pens are poised; was the Brit a cop? No less than 22 Britannias were allocated to Norwich in the late 1950s and by the time this photo was taken, the English Electric Type 4s or Class 40s were making great inroads into the Norwich timetable. Just one year later, all the Norwich services would be diesel hauled. *(Author's Collection)*

INTRODUCTION

In the two years since London's East End Steam was published, a wide variety of new material has come to light from every aspect of the traction spectrum, giving rise to this latest offering from London's East End. The locations contained herein will be familiar to followers of my previous books, but I've taken the liberty of including a couple of views from the wilds of Essex (Shenfield, Upminster and Westcliff) and Hertfordshire (Bishops Stortford), only because they are terrific pictures which will otherwise remain unpublished. Some views are not of the best quality, but they are rare moments in time captured by cameramen with the best equipment and film they possessed at that time. My friend Andy Grimmett has supplied many rare images taken from original negatives which have never been published.

The historical background to London's East End has been well-covered in previous volumes, but the big difference with this volume, is the sheer variety of Motive Power which once graced the area. A brief encounter with the North London line will be found, due to my personal interest. The North London Railway was certainly a trespasser on Great Eastern soil, where it forged an early route to the vast dock network at Poplar. Their locomotive works at Bow was established very early in 1855 but it would never become a serious rival to the giant Stratford Locomotive Works, just over a mile away. Devons Road shed at Bow was the country's very first all diesel depot in 1958, with steam disappearing far too early. Visiting steam did continue however for several years which gave rise to some very interesting pictures of the two forms of traction alongside each other on the Victoria Park to Poplar section. A couple of rare diesel workings on the London Underground Central Line to Epping are included. In the early 1960s it was quite common for special excursion trains to start from Buckhurst Hill or Loughton and head off to the South Coast. These would travel into Liverpool Street via a connection to the BR network at Leyton. Once at Liverpool Street, the locomotive would either run round its train or another locomotive would haul the train back out along the old East London line under the Thames via Surrey Docks to New Cross, then onto the coast.

Moving on to the London Tilbury & Southend lines, some nice views around Barking during construction of the flyover and Ripple Lane have surfaced. Various railtours around the East End have given rise to some rare (even unique) workings and several new views have emerged depicting these. As one would expect, the greatest number of views will of course be Liverpool Street and Stratford, due their sheer popularity with trainspotters and photographers. In Stratford's 160-year history, one of the most interesting periods was the changeover from steam to diesel in the late 1950s. Excluding the early diesel shunters, wholesale introduction of the new order started in earnest with Brush Type 2 D5500 in early November 1957, quickly followed by roughly two more examples every month during 1958. By 1959, Brush Works were building 6-8 Type 2s each month. Hot on the heels of the "Toffee Apples" (D5500-D5519) were the English Electric Type 4s (Class 40s) in the early months of 1958 when D200-D205 arrived to make inroads into the Britannia's on the Norwich service. Several new images have come to light illustrating this brief era.

You might be fortunate enough to have witnessed working steam in the East End prior to September 1962, or perhaps like me, you were a product of the diesel era. Either way, the memories of happier times will come to life again as we tour around familiar old haunts, with steam, diesel, DMU, electric and even a battery loco! I will leave you to wallow in pure nostalgia.

Whilst every effort has been made to ascertain ownership of the pictures, thousands of original negatives change hands every day and occasionally, the ownership gets lost. Those credited to Collections are often unknown and I apologise to anybody who may find their material wrongly credited.

D. Brennand – January 2019

THE NORTH LONDON RAILWAY

Only 30 Class 75 0-6-0T North London Railway tank locomotives were built at Bow Works between 1879 and 1905. Designed for freight shunting, they could occasionally be seen on freight trains, but rarely on passenger services. This is probably the last visit of a NLR built locomotive on a passenger train at Broad Street on 5th May 1956 in the early evening as the LCGB "Poplar & Edgware Tour" finished. Only a handful of the class were left at Devons Road by this time and by 1958 the East End allocation had all been withdrawn. Only No. 58850 soldiered on, with a stay of execution on the Cromford & High Peak Railway in

Derbyshire until 1960, before being preserved. *(Author's Collection)*

A rare sight at Broad Street on 27th April 1958 as the RCTS (London Branch) "Hertfordshire Rail Tour No.2" terminates. This tour originated at Fenchurch Street with another N7 No. 69614 (regular Liverpool Street London Pilot) in charge, but this failed early in the day in the Tottenham area and No. 69632 was found at short notice to replace the failure. The tour visited Harrow & Wealdstone, Stanmore Village and St. Albans Abbey with LMS 2P 0-4-4T No. 41901 in charge and No. 69632 took over from St. Albans Abbey for the remaining section before returning to Broad Street via the

Hertford North to Hertford East connection (closed to all traffic in 1966), then onwards to Stratford and Victoria Park before reaching Broad Street. *(JFS 49 Book Law Publications)*

Few Midland 0-8-0 locomotives ever worked in the area covered by this volume. Broad Street station hosts LNWR G2A class 7F No. 49310, allocated to Bletchley (1E), on 25th February 1956 during shunting operations just outside the station. Substantial goods facilities once existed alongside Broad Street. These locos were collectively known as the 'Super Ds', the last one of which was withdrawn in 1964 and No. 49395 is the only survivor, being part of the National Collection. *(C.J.B. Sanderson/Book Law)*

Freight trains on the Victoria Park to Poplar section were rarely photographed in the dying days of the line. This is Class 31 A1A-A1A No. 31133 (D5551) with a Poplar to Temple Mills working on 9th July 1979. The traffic looks quite healthy with empty steel bogie bolsters and several vans. We are looking towards the site of the old NLR Old Ford station in the distance. Note that the train has a brake van at the front and back, due to the locomotive running round the train at Victoria Park. Freight ended at Poplar Dock in October 1981. *(R. Hummerston)*

Many of the North London Railway stations were built to impress and entice passengers. The architect Edwin Horne designed six of the buildings including Highbury & Islington and Bow, seen here after the upper levels had been removed following a devastating fire in 1957. It had closed to passengers in 1944/5 but soldiered on for another 12 years as a dance hall and billiards club. This view taken in July 1958 is believed to be previously unpublished showing the station frontage on Bow Road after the lower floor had been converted into a BR Parcels Depot, which survived until 1965. The building then stood derelict and was finally demolished in November 1975. *(Author's Collection)*

A locomotive works and engine shed was established by the North London Railway at Bow in 1855. This evolved over many years to become a sprawling site including a carriage works plus associated sidings. The engine shed, which opened in the 1880s, comprised of 20-roads in LNWR days but was reduced to 10 roads in the 1930s. Bow Works employed 700 staff at its height. This is NLR Bow built J.C. Park designed Class 75 (BR 2F) 0-6-0T No. 58856, originally constructed in the 1880s for freight use, at Bow Works minus its side rods in the early 1950s. Of the 30 members in the class, BR inherited half of them at Nationalisation. *(A.F. Grimmett)*

Looking very clean in a freshly applied coat of paint in Bow Works, is LMS "Jinty" 3F 0-6-0 No. 47515 in the late 1950s on Devons Road shed. This locomotive carries the Devons Road 1D shedplate. The largest allocation here in the early 1950s were Jinties, with 40 on the books out of a total allocation of 48 engines. The other eight were a mix of 4Fs and NLR Tanks. After dieselisation of the shed in 1958 No. 47515 found a new lease of life in the North West and was not withdrawn until July 1964. *(Author's Collection)*

Rather scruffy, uncared for and slightly battered NLR 0-6-0T No. 58851 stands alongside Devons Road shed in the mid-1950s. My last visit to the Bluebell Railway in 2017 to see the preserved example (No. 58850) presented me with a very similar view. Considering that historically, this is a very important engine and the only survivor built at Bow Works, its position hidden behind a sales coach at Horsted Keynes, covered in green mould and slowly corroding left me saddened. Hopefully, the custodians of this locomotive will spend some time and money on its restoration and give it

the covered accommodation it rightly deserves so that future generations can enjoy it. *(Author's Collection)*

The axe fell firmly on steam at Devons Road in 1958 and with ruthless efficiency the diesels took over very quickly. This was very much an experiment by BR to prove that it could be done and comply with the London Clean Air Act of 1956, rather than eradicate steam over a period of years, as happened on the rest of the network. Centre stage is North British Loco Company 0-4-0 330 H.P. No. D2903 introduced in 1958 specifically for dock shunting. The first batch (D2900-D2907) were delivered to Devons Road and performed well. For their size, they were powerful and only 20 H.P. less than the BR 08s, but with one less axle. It is hemmed in by the familiar Class 20s and 15s which dominated the motive power scene here. *(Author's Collection)*

None of us has seen a working Class 15 since the class was withdrawn wholesale in 1971. Four were saved as mobile ETH generators and one of those survives (D8233), currently undergoing a full overhaul and restoration at the East Lancs Railway. Introduced in late 1957 and built by the Yorkshire Engine Company in Sheffield, the first batch (D8200-D8209) went to Devons Road. Powered by an 800 H.P. Paxman engine with British-Thompson Houston/AEI electronics, the class was prone to various engine problems, leaks and even fires, all of which should be eradicated when the survivor runs again. An almost new D8201 stands outside Devons Road shed in 1958 being admired (or loathed) by one of the fitters! *(Author's Collection)*

The well-known NLR 0-6-0T Class 75 Park tank locos were a familiar sight around Poplar and Millwall Junction. When the first one was built in 1879, it carried the number 75, hence the classification. The following 30 however were not always numbered consecutively. This was No. 62 built in 1887 at Bow Works and ended its days as BR No. 58852. When fresh out of the works it would have been fully lined. It is oddly carrying its later LMS number 27510, but with an 'M' prefix and BR in full; an interim measure prior to 58852 being applied with the lion over wheel crest. It is seen shunting in Harrow Lane sidings, Poplar on 22nd February 1950. Withdrawal came in June 1955. *(R.A.P. Cogger)*

Drewery class 0-6-0 204 H.P. No. D2217 from Stratford depot is seen climbing the incline by Millwall Junction in 1963. The incline started by Poplar Loop Line box in Harrow Lane sidings and rose to the high level Poplar Dock yard passing Blackwall Bridge signal box. An English Electric Type 1 Bo-Bo is seen in Harrow Lane sidings. The lengthy footbridge spanned all the sidings, Millwall Junction station and led into the PLA exchange sidings for dock employees. *(A. Powell)*

The LCGB "Poplar & Edgware Railtour" coaches sit in Harrow Lane sidings on 5th May 1956 and in good old fashioned pre-Health & Safety style, the passengers were encouraged to swarm all over the place with impunity. Bank signal box is being visited and the Battery Electric Loco No. 1 is parked up and posing in one of its regular sidings. The signal box was of GER design dating back to 1893 and previously carried the names West India Dock Sidings and Millwall Bank. By 1961 the box had closed, and all the signals connected to it were removed. This is not the same view as appeared in LEER Part 2 on page 12 by the late Alan Jackson, as there are different gentlemen on the signal box steps. *(Author's Collection)*

Quite a bit of research went into finding the exact location of this image at Poplar on 19th April 1958. With help from fellow North London Railway Historical Society members, we found that it is Poplar Dock LNWR coal yard. Poplar Central signal box and the former Poplar East India Road station would be behind the photographer and Blackwall Bridge box would be to the right on the embankment. English Electric Type 1 Bo-Bo 1000 H.P. No. D8018 of Devons Road is only two months old and provides the motive power for what appears to be an official brake van tour, but no details have been found of a tour on that date. What a terrific day out; perhaps somebody will recall it? *(Author's Collection)*

This view of Poplar LNWR coal sidings helps explain the location of the previous view. This was taken in the late 1970s and is the less photographed area of the Poplar and Millwall Junction complex. The sidings here were laid in an S shape and originally continued round to the right where they reduced into just four sidings which ran alongside Poplar Dock for loading and unloading onto waiting ships. By the early 1950s, the sidings on the left became dead end and many of the vans seen here would have been in storage, possibly for seasonal traffic. The track on the right continued to the dock. *(J. Connor)*

Class 31 No. 31138 (D5556) shunts brake vans at Poplar on 8th October 1979. Taken from a road bridge, this was a rarely photographed location and overlooked by most enthusiasts, but Roland Hummerston went out of his way to capture rare occurrences and soon to disappear views. Harrow Lane sidings were to the right and Poplar Dock sidings were to the left. The branch from Victoria Park to Poplar was nicknamed 'Bomb Alley' by drivers, as you never knew what would be thrown at you by the local yobs! Over the weekends, when nothing ran, obstacles including old kitchen appliances would often be gathered on the track to greet us on the first trip on Monday mornings. *(R. Hummerston)*

Excited enthusiasts (no, its not a modern phenomenon), hang out of the windows as the "East London Railtour", organised by The Railway Enthusiasts Club enters Millwall Junction (Poplar) from the North London line on 26th August 1961. The train was hauled throughout by LMS Ivatt class 2 2-6-0 No. 46472. Enfield (GN), Palace Gates and even Thames Haven were on the itinerary that day. West India Docks are in the background and a Devons Road Class 20 is fussing about in Harrow Lane sidings. My fascination with this area has evolved into reproducing it in model form. *(Author's Collection)*

Following on from the previous view, this is Millwall Junction in OO gauge! Over two years work and far from finished, this is the view from Harrow Lane sidings looking towards Millwall Junction station (closed 1926). The signal box is entirely scratchbuilt, as is the other one on the left; Blackwall Bridge. The station building, lengthy footbridge and platforms are all scratchbuilt too. The track layout has been altered slightly to give continuous running over a large figure-of-eight loop. *(Author)*

GREAT EASTERN SUBURBAN

It is well documented that the arrival of the Britannias on main line services out of Liverpool Street in 1951 caused problems with the length of the new locomotives. This view of a virtually new No. 70003 "John Bunyan" being turned on 20th September 1951, illustrates the problem of overhanging, even after the turntable had been lengthened the previous April. The drivers were very skilled in balancing the loco dead centre and have equal overhang at both ends. *(A.F. Grimmett Collection)*

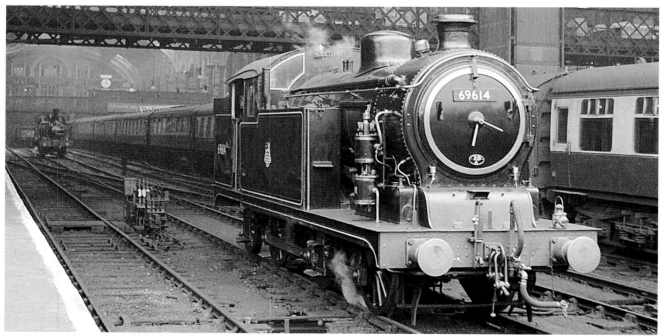

Looking resplendent and highly polished, N7/4 0-6-2T No. 69614 poses on its usual oily patch, 10A road, awaiting its next job during March 1957. This was the West Side pilot and standby engine for N.E. London services. The long-standing tradition dating back to the Great Eastern days, was that the driver and fireman would receive one hour's overtime for cleaning and polishing the London Pilot. A task which carried on in the diesel era with the 08 diesel shunters. *(A.F. Grimmett Collection)*

There was often enough shunting work at Liverpool Street to warrant a second Pilot engine, which was also a standby loco for the East London line. Here is "Buckjumper" J69/1 0-6-0T No. 68619 on just such a turn. Cheerfully posing in front are George Chittenden (seniority 1944) on the left and Albert Cook (seniority 1943). Both men could have been either passed firemen or young drivers, in this mid-1950s view. Both were still drivers at Stratford when I joined BR in 1973. Truly a job for life. *(Author's Collection)*

A triumph of engineering; Britannia class 7P6F 4-6-2 No. 70009 "Alfred the Great" reverses out of Platform 12 at Liverpool Street into the loco sidings in August 1957. Most of us can only dream of what it would have been like to travel behind one of these impressive goliaths on the Norwich main line. New to Norwich on 4th May 1951, it spent a short spell on the Southern later that year, before returning to Norwich until 1961 when it then spent

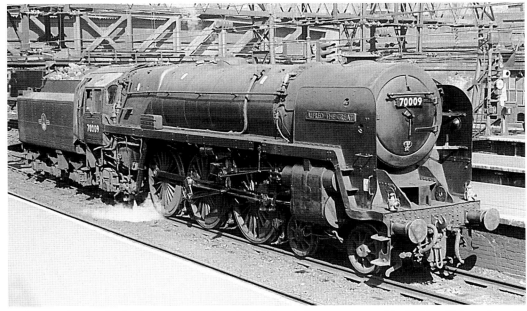

two years at March (31B) before seeing out its final days on the London Midland. It was scrapped in 1967, with less than 16 years' service, which seems wasteful, but this was the harsh brutality of eradicating steam. *(Author's Collection)*

The West Side hosts a particularly clean Thompson L1 2-6-4T 4MT No. 67770 in December 1957 after being released from Stratford Works where records show that it had been under repair since November. It is on a running-in turn before being returned to its home shed, Kings Cross (34A). The first L1 (LNER 9000) entered traffic at Stratford in 1945 and underwent trials for three years until a further batch of 29 were built at Darlington from 1948. Another 70 would eventually enter traffic. Early trial indications from No. 9000 indicated good riding qualities, so it is rather ironic that crews nicknamed them "Cement Mixers"! *(Author's Collection)*

Captured from one of the most famous of all vantage points at Liverpool Street, the taxi rank, is Britannia 7P6F 4-6-2 No. 70002 "Geoffrey Chaucer" in Platform 9 as it backs onto a Norwich train in 1957. The grime, choking smoke, noise and smell would have bombarded the senses, but something called "The Clean Air Act" in 1955 would soon put a stop to all this nonsense! In June 1961 No. 70002 would leave East Anglia for respite in a more steam friendly locality, namely Carlisle Kingmoor (12A), where it would faithfully serve for another six years until withdrawal in March 1967. *(Book Law Publications)*

An impressive sight, but does it beat a Britannia? Not performance wise, but this was the new diesel dawn at Liverpool Street on 31st May 1958, as English Electric Type 4 1Co-Co1 2000 H.P. No. D202 almost fresh off the production line, prepares to assault the Norwich main line. Generations of steam enthusiasts would no doubt shed a few tears, but the shiny green monster and its descendants were here to stay; well, for the next 30-odd years anyway! Try to find a diesel loco at Liverpool Street today. The old Gresley coach behind the Type 4 in blood and custard livery is a delightful contrast. *(C.J.B. Sanderson/Book Law Publications)*

Built by the LNER at Darlington in 1931 to Sir Nigel Gresley's rather pleasing design was B17/3 4-6-0 No. 61631 "Serlby Hall", named after the home of Viscount Galway near Retford. It was first allocated to Stratford, but moved around various East Anglian sheds, except for a brief spell at Doncaster in 1934. From 1953 until its demise it was an Ipswich (32B) engine. It is seen here on the turntable at Liverpool Street in 1958, having been rebuilt as a B17/3 the previous year. A great shame that just one year later it would be condemned and cut up at Doncaster. *(A.F. Grimmett Collection)*

The scale of a Britannia is evident when the human element is alongside. No. 70005 "John Milton" has been turned and is being prepared for the task ahead. This engine was new to Stratford on 1st January 1951 and stayed for two years before being transferred to Norwich (32A). Upon the end of steam in East Anglia it was transferred to the London Midland where it stayed until being withdrawn in July 1967. It was scrapped at Campbell's in Airdrie the following year. *(Book Law Publications)*

The year of 1962 was truly momentous for railway enthusiasts and Norwich City supporters! LNER Thompson designed Class B1 4-6-0 No. 61286 stands in the dark depths of 10 Dock at Liverpool Street in April 1962, the year that Norwich City won the Football League Cup. They beat Rochdale 4-0 over two matches on 26th April and 1st May, which helps date the picture. We will never know who was responsible for the adornment on the smokebox door, but it certainly gives the front end a bit of character. The engine is a Cambridge (31A) loco and lasted right up to the end of East Anglian steam, eventually being withdrawn on 16th September 1962. *(Author's Collection)*

Majestic and powerful looking, English Electric Type 4 1Co-Co1 2000 H.P. D203 (40003) stands on the centre road in Liverpool Street loco sidings on 22nd June 1958, just one month after entering service. D200–D205 all started their careers at Stratford between March and June 1958, as a planned dieselisation of the Norwich services. A friend who is now in his 80s left the footplate after the Type 4s came along in 1958. "Give me a Brit on a Norwich any day" he said. *(A.F. Grimmett Collection)*

You can almost sense the excitement that this young lad would have felt on seeing his first glimpse of a virtually new BR Sulzer Type 2 Bo-Bo 1160 H.P. No. D5020 at Liverpool Street on 6th September 1959 working a class 2 passenger train. The loco had only entered traffic a few weeks previously and was initially allocated to Ipswich (32B). This is one of my favourite views of a diesel at Liverpool Street. The long-lost age of innocence and wonderment, free of Health & Safety intrusion. Today's management would no doubt shut the station if any youngster stood so close to the platform edge. Perhaps he had common sense. *(Author's Collection)*

Fresh out of Brush Works, Loughborough is Brush Type 2 A1A-A1A 1470 H.P. No. D5549 (31131) on 19th September 1959, after just nine days in service. The paintwork is immaculate; no wonder that the photographers were out in force to capture these revolutionary locomotives, which heralded an exciting new age in motive power. Ipswich (32B) was its first shed and various other reallocations followed. It was not until late 1971 that it came to Stratford, but that only lasted four months. It was withdrawn in March 1989 and cut up by Berry's of Leicester in early 1990. *(A.F. Grimmett Collection)*

Something that would have been an everyday occurrence at Liverpool Street prior to the end of steam in September 1962, but rarely captured on film. English Electric Type 3 Co-Co 1750 H.P. No. D6707 (37007) is being moved on the turntable to access one of the engine sidings. New to March (31B) depot in February 1961, this loco moved to Stratford in 1963 and stayed there for a further four years. *(Unknown/ Author's Collection)*

The transition from steam to diesel was quick and ruthless, with hundreds of locos being dispatched very quickly to the breakers. On the positive side though, there were photographic opportunities arising with the new forms of traction from the same familiar haunts that previous generations had used. The taxi rank approach road at Liverpool Street was one of the best-known spotting haunts ever. Our cameraman has captured five-week old English Electric Type 3 Co-Co 1750 H.P. No D6718 on 15th July 1961 about to work a Down Road express. Steam is still around, but there is not a wisp of it here. *(A.F. Grimmett Collection)*

The BR Board must have regretted the decision to order over 125 diesel locomotives from the North British Locomotive Company (excluding some of the WR Warships) in the late 1950s as many of them were unreliable when compared to other manufacturers. The company was successful at steam loco building but that did not carry over into the diesel era. Poor Stratford staff had the ten NBL Type 1 Bo-Bo 800 H.P. (Class 16s) thrust upon them in 1958, but ten years later they were relieved when the whole class was

withdrawn. They had the same Paxman 16YHXL engine as the BTH (Class 15) but for some reason they were even more problematic in the NBL locos. The single Gresley coach should not be too much of a challenge for D8400 at Liverpool Street's Platform 10 in the mid-1960s. *(Book Law Publications)*

Those of us that are of a certain vintage will remember Class 20s 'whistling while they worked' at Liverpool Street, either on empty stock workings or the London Pilot. This is such a beast, No. D8056 (20056), one of the last three remaining at Stratford in the early 1970s. It is on the London Pilot job on this occasion, about to shunt the stock from Platform 9 to release the engine at the other end. *(Author's Collection)*

There are just a handful of spotters in this view, but it belies the fact that Liverpool Street was a haven for those of us who pursued such a harmless pastime. Over the 130-odd years of its existence, there must have been millions of us! Today's station offers far less in the way of traction or variety, and sadly, those in charge often deem it suspicious or a security issue that somebody would want to stand on the end of a platform and collect train numbers! Soak up the arrival of a Class 309, No. 605 with an inbound service from Clacton in 1973. *(Author's Collection)*

"Toffee Apple" Brush Type 2 A1A-A1A 1470 H.P. No. 31004 (D5504) waits patiently on the buffers in Platform 7 after being uncoupled from its train on 22nd June 1977. It had most likely brought in empty stock, as Toffee Apples were rarely trusted to work mainline express services by this stage in their careers. I did once work a Norwich train with one in the 1970s, due to the failure of a 47 when there was nothing else available. We had lost about 20 minutes by the time we arrived in Norwich. (R. Hummerston)

The only EMUs to ever carry main line maroon livery were the superbly styled AM9 (Class 309) units built at York between 1962/3. Only 23 units were constructed, and their build quality, good riding and comfort made them an instant success on the Liverpool Street to Clacton and Walton services. This is one of the eight two-car units, No. 607 at Thornton Fields carriage sidings in 1963. They served Essex commuters very well for over 25 years. (Author's Collection)

BR built "Baby Sulzer" Type 2 Bo-Bo 1160 H.P. No. D5028 was new to Ipswich (32B) depot in November 1959. It is seen passing through Stratford with a Class 3 Empty Stock working on 8th August 1960. This loco would never receive its TOPS number, as it was destroyed at Chester General station whilst working a tanker train from Ellesmere Port to Mold Junction after running out of control on 8th May 1972. (R. Hummerston)

Pictures of Britannias working on the GE are quite common, but this is a rare shot taken on 26th January 1959 of No. 70013 "Oliver Cromwell" running light engine out of Thornton Fields carriage sidings between Bow Junction and Stratford. Apologies for the camera shake, but the photographer is obviously in a moving train on the Up Electric line. The sidings were torn up in 2008 to make way for the Olympic Stadium site and 70013 is of course now preserved. *(Author's Collection)*

Brush Type 2 No. D5619 (31195) passes through Stratford with an Up Road express on 8th August 1960. New to Stratford in May 1960, this loco only saw service until February 1988 and was cut up by Booth's of Rotherham the following September. Around 26 members of this highly popular class have been preserved. Two of the latest to be saved in October 2018 are 31105/D5523 and 31233/D5660, which have been sold by Network Rail to Mangapps Farm Railway Museum in Essex. *(R. Hummerston)*

Hopefully images like this will live on in our minds and in print. This was an age of innocence, when parents thought nothing of letting their offspring spend the day on a railway station, miles from home, collecting loco numbers; you had to be there. A gaggle of spotters witness British-Thompson Houston Type 1 Bo-Bo 800 H.P. No D8210 running through Stratford light engine on 8th August 1960. This was the first of the Pioneer examples to arrive new at Stratford in November 1959, as the previous ten had gone to Devons Road. It was withdrawn in March 1971, stored at Ipswich for six months and cut up at Crewe Works in March 1972. *(R. Hummerston)*

Another Stratford BTH (Class 15) Type 1 No. D8232 waits patiently for the road via Channelsea curve with a Temple Mills bound freight in 1962. This loco entered service in August 1960 and was first shedded at Norwich (32A). Just one month later it came to Stratford where it would stay for the next three years. After withdrawal in March 1971 it was also stored at the closed Ipswich (32B) depot for several months with many of its classmates before being cut up at Crewe Works the following October. *(Author's Collection)*

From 1986 the branch line from Manningtree to Harwich Parkeston Quay was electrified, enabling electric loco haulage of the Boat Trains. This is "The European" from Harwich Parkeston Quay to Glasgow via the North London line and the WCML. Class 47 No. 47475 (D1603) has just been attached to the front of the Class 86 at Channelsea Junction for haulage over the North London line, which was only electrified with the third rail system. Upon arrival at Willesden, the diesel would be taken off. Stratford did not provide motive power for this service. They once lost a 47 for a week after it set off on this service! *(Author's Collection)*

Standing outside Stratford New Shed during a shift change of Engine Repair Shop staff is F5 (GER M15) 2-4-2T No. 7210 (7109/67210) in late 1949. The K3 2-6-0 No. 61830 has its BR number, but the F5 was not renumbered to No. 67210 until 14th January 1950. The type of passenger work that the F5/F6s were employed on were increasingly being taken over by N7 0-6-2Ts. By 1958 the whole class had been withdrawn and this example only lasted until 4th July 1955 when it was withdrawn and cut up at Stratford. *(A.F. Grimmett Collection)*

The first LNER Thompson L1 2-6-4T No. 9000 had entered service in 1945, but there was a lull of three years until production commenced on the rest of the class. No. 67711 was built in 1948, but painted LNER Apple Green, as were the following engines up to 67722. It is seen at Stratford early in its stay, as it was reallocated to Ipswich in May 1950. The connecting rod, some of the valve gear and a cylinder cover have been removed for maintenance. No. 67723 was the first one to emerge from Darlington in BR lined black. *(A.F. Grimmett Collection)*

Such was the complexity of Stratford depot and works in its heyday, that a thorough tour could take up to two hours. Tucked away in one of the many nooks and crannies is E4 (GER T26) 2-4-0 No. 62780 from Cambridge (31A) in 1955 awaiting the cutter's torch. Of the 100 built by the GER between 1891 and 1902, only 18 were left in service upon Nationalisation in 1948. This was the lowest BR numbered E4 and the oldest that survived into BR ownership, built in April 1891 at Stratford as GER number 427. It was condemned in September 1955 and cut up on site. *(Book Law Publications)*

Geoff Silcock mentioned in his Foreword for London's East End Steam how the J69 "Buckjumper" 0-6-0T No. 8568 (68568) was overlooked at Stratford for many years after Nationalisation and carried its LNER number right up until April 1956 before finally getting its BR number. Here it is in 1955 by the coal stage still clearly showing No. 8568 seven years after the formation of BR. This was the last steam engine to carry an LNER number at Stratford and possibly on the entire Eastern Region. Its fame was short-lived though; by May 1958 it was withdrawn and cut up on site. *(A.F. Grimmett Collection)*

The combination of the BR Modernisation Plan and The Clean Air Act in 1955 would have put a bit of a black cloud over the future of steam in London and the East End was first in line for the cull of steam power. The appearance of some of the smaller shunting engines was not a priority, although passenger locos were kept clean, the numerous yard and shed pilots became very scruffy. This is J69 No. 68630 in 1955 sporting the early BR lion over wheel emblem, just about visible under the grime. The new diesels sealed its fate and it was condemned on 1st January 1959. *(A.F. Grimmett Collection)*

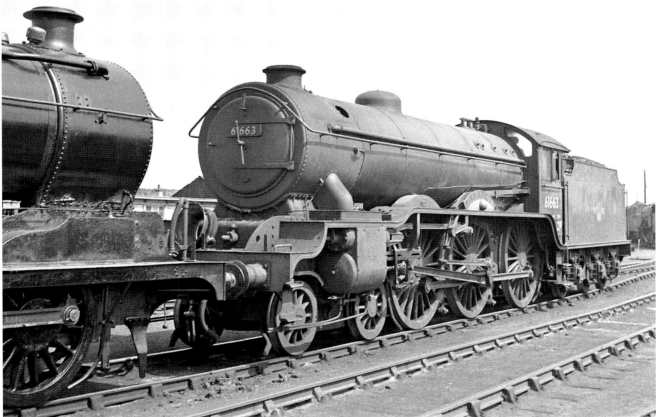

Few locomotives that worked in the East End were so charismatic and respected as the B17/6 4-6-0 "Footballers". Whether or not you are a football fan, the locomotives certainly had their fans too. This is No. 61663 "Everton" on shed at Stratford on 31st May 1955. Several unreadable chalked comments appear on the cabside; could they be from Everton fans or their opponents? Built for the LNER by Robert Stephenson & Hawthorn Co. Ltd at their Darlington Works in 1937, this was one of eleven B17s constructed by RS&H Ltd. It carries a 30A shedplate as it was allocated here four times during its existence. It was allocated here in February 1960 when condemned and later cut up at Doncaster. *(Book Law Publications)*

Stratford born and bred J69/1 (GER R24) "Buckjumper" class 0-6-0T No. 68532 is truly dwarfed by the giant coal stage in this 1955 view. Some poor souls would have worked inside the coaling facility, which must have been one dirty and arduous job. This loco was withdrawn from revenue earning service in December 1958 and transferred into loco departmental stock, being renumbered as Dept. No.43 in January 1959, which only lasted until August 1959 when it was condemned and cut up at Stratford. *(Book Law Publications)*

J15 class 0-6-0 No. 65468 stands at Stratford on 26th February 1956 with a visitor off the GN lines in the shape of an N2 0-6-2T No. 69521 minus its cab during repairs in the Engine Repair Shop in the background. As a class Y14 in GER days, this engine entered service in 1912, spending its career at several East Anglian sheds. It was withdrawn in September 1959 and met its maker where it was constructed. The GER built no less than 289 of these fine-looking engines at Stratford (except for nineteen built by Sharp, Stewart & Co.) between 1883 and 1913 specifically for freight. *(A.F. Grimmett Collection)*

There are no prizes for guessing what this lot are up to. One of many organised trainspotters trips around Stratford depot in the 1950s. What a privilege to be so up close and personal with so many working engines. Some of us can only imagine the excitement, sounds and smells. Centre stage is Stratford allocated J15 (GER Y14) 0-6-0 No. 65445, which lasted until August 1962. It was cut up by Kings near Brunswick Junction, Poplar in March 1964. *(Author's Collection)*

The great new diesel dawn at Stratford on 29th June 1958. Pioneer D200 (40122) and D204 (40004) stand outside the only diesel facilities available. The later B&C sheds would not open for another three years. This shed would be used for DMU servicing in later years. The lack of high-level platforms inside the shed hampered maintenance of the early arrivals. The English Electric Vulcan Factory churned out the first six members of the class to Stratford between March and June 1958, making D204 brand new when photographed. They were quickly put to work on Norwich services. Some crews were pleased to see them, but others were less enthusiastic. Present day Class 40 fans might find that hard to believe! *(A.F. Grimmett Collection)*

Andrew Barclay 1956 built 0-4-0 153 H.P. No. 11505 (D2955/01002) stands outside Stratford New Shed on 9th August 1958. Ideally suited for working around the East End yards, there were only five locos in the class. Amazingly, this one along with 11504 (D2954/01001), found further use on the isolated Holyhead breakwater line and received TOPS numbers (01001/2) in 1974. Both survived until 1982, when they were scrapped on site. Fortunately, D2953 and D2956 survive in preservation. *(Author's Collection)*

A very early diesel interloper at Stratford on 29th June 1958 was this new German Waggon & Maschinenbau 4-wheel railbus No. 79962 destined for the Witham – Maldon line. Only five were built and they came into the UK via Harwich. This may well have been on its way to Cambridge depot where they were based. Their use on the Maldon line was only of limited success as they had too few seats (just 56) to cope with peak demands. Four out of the five survive including this one at the Keithley & Worth Valley Railway. *(Author's Collection)*

The quirky little (GER B74) Y4 0-4-0 A.J. Hill tanks were always synonymous with Stratford from 1913 until 1963 when 68129 (No. 33) was finally withdrawn. Only five were ever built at Stratford. This is No. 68127 captured on shed in 1956 standing in front of N7 0-6-2T No. 69713. Note the dumb wooden buffers to combat buffer locking on tight bends. There was barely any room in the cab for coal, so it was stored on top of the firebox; a bit of a design flaw there! *(A.F. Grimmett Collection)*

Capturing new images of three out of the five Y4's is not a bad achievement. These were powerful little engines for their relatively small size and terrifically robust, designed for working around tight radius curves at Canning Town and Mile End. This example, pictured at Stratford, No. 68128 was built in 1921 and was one of three Y4s to be withdrawn in 1955/6. *(Author's Collection)*

The Stratford Shed Pilot with chalked nickname "Noddy", after the well-known Enid Blyton character, is seen behind the New Shed on 11th February 1961. We can safely assume that the nickname came from the rocking motion as the 38 ton loco moved over uneven low-quality track. Originally built by the GER in 1913 as a B74, it became a Y4 under LNER ownership. In BR days it gained the number 68129, then No. 33 once in Departmental use. It was the last working steam loco at Stratford. The driver is believed to be Bill Webb. *(A.F. Grimmett Collection)*

The Drewery Car Company built 140 small 204 H.P. 0-6-0 shunting locomotives for BR over a period of ten years starting in 1952. This example No. 11131 is pictured on shed at Stratford, its first shed when entering service in October 1955 and still carrying its original black livery in early 1959. It was renumbered D2225 in September 1959 and was withdrawn from BR service in 1969 but saw further service with the National Coal Board at Wath until 1985 when it was cut up. *(A.F. Grimmett Collection)*

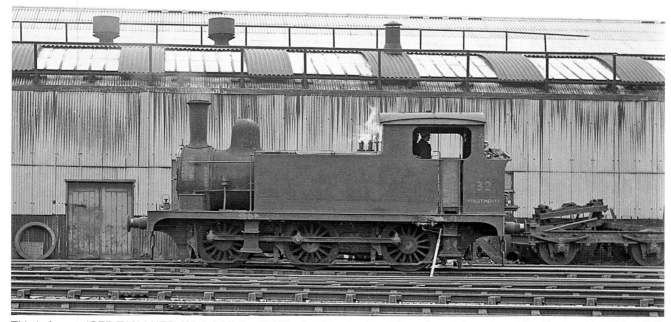

This is former (GER T18) LNER J66 0-6-0T No. 68370 after it had entered Departmental service at Stratford as No. 32 in 1955. This was the very last member of a class of 50 locos to be in service and none survive. Dating back to 1886, eleven of these engines (which were designated shunting locos), had Westinghouse brakes fitted and worked briefly on the Enfield and Chingford services. It is pictured alongside the carriage sheds by Chobham Farm Junction on 19th May 1962. *(Author's Collection)*

COLOUR SECTION

Of all the forms of East End Traction, this rates as the most unusual. One of only two built; one by the North Staffordshire Railway (BEL No. 2), now preserved by the NRM, and BEL No. 1 built by the Midland Railway in 1914 at Derby, specifically for use in West India Dock coal depot as seen here in the mid-1950s. The coal depot was at a lower level and could only be reached via a wagon hoist. The battery electric loco fitted on the hoist and the wagon turntables. It was withdrawn in 1964 and scrapped by Kings of Norwich. *(Steam & Sail)*

This lovely low-relief map of the complex railway system around Poplar Dock is part of the National Railway Museum Collection. This fascinating area of true East End Docklands would have been a most frantic hive of activity until the mid-1960s when rail-born freight traffic started to lose out to road competition and the rival ports, particularly Tilbury. Apart from the Great Eastern and North London Railways having goods facilities here, the Great Northern, Midland and even the Great Western all had their own goods depots.

A visit by the RCTS on 21st October 1967 to Millwall Junction (Harrow Lane Sidings) used a 6-car Met-Cam DMU. The tour started from Fenchurch Street and visited Barking, Tilbury, Thames Haven, South Tottenham, High Meads, Victoria Park, Poplar, Bow (NL), reversing, then via the curve to Gas Factory Junction and Fenchurch Street, making it the last ever passenger train to use the curve. The junction was severed in December 1967. *(J. Connor)*

Celebrity status was bestowed upon J69 (GER S56) "Buckjumper" 0-6-0T No. 68619 in the 1950s when it became one of two regular London Pilots; the other being N7 0-6-2T No. 69614. In 1959 it was repainted at Stratford into beautifully lined GER Royal Blue livery, complete with the ornate GER crest. It is captured moving out of siding 9A at Liverpool Street on 16th May 1961. In the background sits an unidentified "Britannia", where some poor soul has been given the task of moving the coal forward in the tender – any volunteers? *(Author's Collection)*

A rather grubby AM2 (302) 4-car Fenchurch Street - Shoeburyness line EMU No. 238 stands at Liverpool Street in the early 1960s. Building of these units began in 1958 and 112 were eventually in service with some lasting until 1997/8. So many came out of the works in the early 1960s (before the LT&SR electrification had been completed), that they were drafted onto GE metals until required on the Tilbury and Shoeburyness routes. *(B. Harrison/North Norfolk Railway)*

Normally associated with the LT&SR line is another Class 302, No. 287 standing in Platform 5 at Liverpool Street in 1964. To the left is a freight wagon, possibly part of a parcels train. The delightful BR Green with half yellow ends was one of the most attractive ever carried on EMU stock; I am not so sure about the early attempt at hi-viz with the orange handrails though! It is interesting to remember that there was no front illumination apart from the headcode and destination boxes. *(Unknown/Author's Collection)*

The British Transport Commission of 1955 demanded that steam would be eradicated over several years by the introduction of approximately 2500 new diesels, some of which were completely untested. Along came the British Thompson-Houston Type 1s with their 800 H.P. Paxman engines, which in the long-term proved to be their downfall, due to leaks, piston seizures and general unreliability limiting their usefulness. As a design, however, they were certainly an attractive looking loco, but even this had an aspect that the designers overlooked or ignored. The

view from the tiny cab windows when running with the long bonnet first gave very restricted visibility on bends. All that aside, just soak up the pure nostalgia of D8234 on the Liverpool Street London Pilot turn on 5th April 1964. *(J. Boyes/Book Law)*

You don't learn how to drive trains by just sitting in a classroom. My early days as a Secondman were an apprenticeship covering a five year period until I was old enough to become a driver. I worked gradually through the 16 links at Stratford, ending up in the Norwich gang at the tender age of 20. My regular driver in that gang was Dick Cumberworth, shown here posing for an official photographer on one of two specially adorned Class 47s, No. 47164 that carried a Union Jack to commemorate the Queen's Silver Jubilee during 1977. The other locomotive was No. 47163. Dick was a real character, practical joker and a very fine tutor. I would often drive to Norwich under his gaze and he would bring the train back. The renowned railway historian and author O.S. Nock once had the pleasure of a cab ride with Dick and recalled that he had never laughed so much! *(Author's Collection)*

(*left*) Poking its nose out of the gloom that was 10 Dock next to Platform 10 at Liverpool Street in the early 1970s is Class 37 No. 37109 (D6809). This was one of the less salubrious areas of the station. Years of oil leakages and general waste would gather here, plus the inevitable trainspotters. As D6809, this loco was new to Darnall (Sheffield) in 1963. From the mid-1970s until 1987 it was allocated to March (31B), and so became a frequent visitor to Liverpool Street on Cambridge loco hauled services. It is now owned by an ex-Stratford driver and can be found working on the East Lancs Railway. *(Author's Collection)*

(*below*) An unidentified Class 47 sits in the loco holding sidings by Platform 10 in 1981. This would not have been a Stratford engine for sure, as the cleaners would have got a rollicking! The headcode 4E60 indicates that it had previously worked a Freightliner train to the Eastern Region from either the Western or Midland Region. Class 37 No. 37017 (D6717) keeps it company. *(Author's Collection)*

Some pictures are so striking that they capture a moment in time perfectly. You can sense the noise and vibrations of the idling Sulzer engine, the smell of the oil and diesel, not to mention the jealous feelings towards the lucky crew. This is Class 47 No. 47169 (D1764), newly named "Great Eastern" in March 1979. The loco carried this name until August 1990. It was renumbered 47581 in December 1979 and 47763 in December 1993. Withdrawal came in November 2000 and scrapping took place at Motherwell in 2003. *R. Hummerston)*

A very grey 1st March 1980 is brightened up by the rare visit of an HST set to Liverpool Street forming a special service to celebrate 100 years of the London Tilbury & Southend Railway. The train ran to Southend Central via Woodgrange Park and Barking. It was well patronised and well photographed, as a real one-off occasion. Thankfully, despite the units now being over 40 years old, some ex-GWR sets are seeing a new lease of life in Scotland as reformed 4 and 5 car sets. With over 4500 H.P. and short trains, there are exciting prospects ahead. *(Author's Collection)*

The very rare sight of a Class 45 "Peak" No. 45119 (D34) in Liverpool Street loco sidings on 13th November 1982. It had worked the Hertfordshire Railtours "Ouse Crouch Crusader" from Bedford and spent the whole day here, before working the train back to Bedford later in the afternoon. Both 47576 and 37075 also worked the railtour, which visited Enfield Town, Southminster and Chingford. When built in July 1961 at Derby Works, D34 was the 1000th main line diesel locomotive to enter service on BR. *(Author's Collection)*

This is a rarely photographed trip working into Liverpool Street with fuel for the loco sidings. Taken in September 1984, Class 37 No. 37055 (D6755) is entering Platform 10, where the tanks would be propelled back into the sidings. This loco spent many years working around the North East at Gateshead and Thornaby, but came to Stratford in January 1981, where it stayed until 1989. It was withdrawn in December 2007 and scrapped at Kingsbury in April 2008. In the background is 47582 (D1765/47160) "County of Norfolk". *(Author's Collection)*

A most unusual series of special trains titled "The Ford Executive" were laid on by the Ford Motor Company in April 1985. The Class 31s chosen for the task were 31409, 31412, 31416 and 31430. They ran from Liverpool Street to Witham for a press event at Boreham House. This is 31416 (D5842) about to depart on 16th April 1985. *(B. Dann)*

Not just any old 350 H.P. 08 diesel shunter would do for the London Pilot. Several played the role over the years, including 08833 (D4001) which was painted GER Royal Blue by Stratford of course. Long into the BR Blue era, 08531 (D3693) was repainted back into BR Green with the old BR Lion over Wheel emblem. It looks incredibly smart when captured in 1986 standing in Platform 10. The Stratford driver on the left is Kenny White, who can only just be seen, but his distinctive beard is a giveaway to anybody who knew him. *(Author's Collection)*

One of the pleasures of driving trains is the panoramic view from the cab, as is perfectly illustrated here. The driver of a train standing on the Up Electric line at Bishopsgate captures a Class 309 Clacton set with No. 624 leading, as it departs from Liverpool Street on 1st October 1985. It is attached to another in Jaffa Cake livery. On the left is the erstwhile platform of Bishopsgate Low Level, which closed in May 1916. To the right is the towering edifice of the former Bishopsgate goods depot which burnt down in 1964. The remains of the depot are a Listed Structure. *(B. Dann)*

The glory days of Class 40s out of Liverpool Street were recreated on 9th May 1987 when Hertfordshire Railtours ran their "Anglian Diesel Farewell" tour with D200 (40122) and 37138. Having just departed from London, it is approaching Bethnal Green cautiously, as it will be taking the sharp curve towards Hackney Downs. The first destination was Kings Lynn, then Bury St. Edmunds, Ipswich, (Harwich Town, Lowestoft, Norwich behind 37138) and a final onslaught on the main line back to Liverpool Street behind D200. One superb day out for all those lucky enough to have got tickets. *(G. Silcock)*

As the Lea Valley line was not originally scheduled for electrification, when the Bishops Stortford to Hackney Downs line via Lower Edmonton, Enfield Town and Chingford branches were equipped with overhead lines, there was a need for DMUs to bridge the gap between Coppermill Junction and Cheshunt. The 20 Rolls Royce engined Class 125 Derby built units were built from 1958 specifically for the Lea Valley line. This example is approaching Cambridge Heath in 1961 with a Liverpool Street to Cheshunt service. The Lea Valley line was eventually electrified in 1969. *(Author's Collection)*

Brush Type 2 A1A-A1A 1470 H.P. No. D5595 (31175), a Stratford (30A) engine, works an Up Road Loughton to Brighton special through Stratford station on 15th July 1962. This came off the Epping line via the connections at Leyton and Temple Mills East. This loco was new to Hornsey (34B) in March 1960 and came to Stratford in March 1961. It was withdrawn in March 1987 and cut up at Carlisle Kingmoor in July 1988. *(Author's Collection)*

All sorts of weird and wonderful sights could be enjoyed at Stratford station. A rare visitor from the Southern is Class 33 BRCW Type 3 1550 H.P. No. 33101 (D6511) passing eastwards through Stratford in the 1980s. It is probably working a special, hauling a SR 4TC set No. 8030. These were unpowered units normally found between Waterloo and Weymouth. Note that there is no third rail pick up gear on the bogies. *(Author's Collection)*

LMS "Jinty" 3F 0-6-0 No. 47467 from Camden (1B) depot heads a freight from the Midland Region towards the docks through Stratford Low Level circa 1950. The driver would have the regulator open wide here to keep the couplings tight and stop the train snatching as it descends then rises quickly under the GE main line in the background. This was a common problem with loose-coupled freight and we were told very early in our careers to watch out for it. A severe snatch could break couplings or give the guard a very rough ride! *(Steam & Sail)*

The opening of the North London line connection between Dalston Eastern Junction and Stratford Low Level to regular passenger traffic on 14th May 1979 proved very popular and quickly exceeded the expected passenger numbers. Today the line carries thousands of passengers per hour. The existing North Woolwich service was extended to Camden Road, running at 30-minute intervals. This Cravens Class 105 has arrived at Stratford Low Level from Camden Road circa 1980. *(Author's Collection)*

These were a pleasure to drive. Built like a tank and with superb traditional tread brakes with cast iron brake blocks. Designed originally during the LNER years, their introduction was delayed by the Second World War and the fleet comprising of 92 AM6 (306) Liverpool Street – Shenfield units entered service in 1949, serving East End and Essex commuters faithfully for over 30 years. This image was taken on 11th February 1980 at Stratford, the final year of service as the new 315s were introduced from 1979 onwards; one of which can be seen in the Old Yard. *(Author's Collection)*

Some interesting and long-forgotten information came to light whilst researching this image of Class 37 No. 37099 (D6799) heading west through Stratford on 2nd October 1980, with what appears to be a short parcels train. Some friends rallied round and found out that it is in fact a train sponsored by The Shaftesbury Society for the poor, disabled and underprivileged to visit Dovercourt Bay near Harwich for a holiday. This is the return working in the late afternoon. The BG parcels van was used for wheelchairs. *(A.F. Grimmett Collection)*

Class 31 A1A-A1A Type 2 No. 31199 (D5623) trundles over Stratford Central Junction in the early 1980s with a train of Distillers carbon dioxide tanks for Bow Midland yard. This engine was variously allocated to Finsbury Park and Stratford during its career, which ended in May 2000, being cut up at Stockton three years later. *(Author's Collection)*

A view of double-headed Class 37s with 37070 (D6770) leading on a freight passing through Stratford heading towards Temple Mills via Channelsea curve. This image would have been taken between 1982-4, as 37070 was briefly allocated to Stratford at this time. It was a long-time Tyneside engine with spells at Gateshead and Thornaby, where it returned in May 1984. It was stored at Doncaster and Toton during the 1990s, and whilst at Toton it was allocated Departmental No. ADB68036 (unpowered power unit carrier), although it never actually carried this number. It was cut up at Toton in 2004. *(Author's Collection)*

The spectacle of Class 47 Co-Co 2750 H.P. No 47568 (D1626/47045) in full flight in the early 1980s, as the driver opens the controller to full throttle after negotiating the junction at the east end of Stratford station with a Norwich to Liverpool Street express. The scream of a 47 is still as exciting today on several preserved railways, but rarely will one attain the speeds of the Glory Days depicted here, unless it is one of the few main line certified examples. *(Author's Collection)*

The clanking couplings and buffers, screeching of flanges on tight bends and the Class 37 roaring away at the front. What more do you want? Powering off Channelsea curve at Stratford is Class 37 Co-Co 1750 H. P. No. 37057 (D6757) in the early 1980s with the classic 16-ton minerals in tow full of coal. The move away from the burning of fossil fuel has seen this type of traffic disappear, making hundreds of freight drivers redundant over recent years. *(Author's Collection)*

Traction? Perhaps; the once-familiar self-propelled steam cranes would occasionally been seen with one or two wagons attached. This delightful image taken on 26th July 1964 at Stratford during track relaying work, shows 10 ton Grafton Travelling Steam Crane No. DB966271 in full flight. This was built in 1952 and allocated to Leyton Depot. It was scrapped in 1982. Roughly two years after the end of steam at Stratford, the sight and sound of working steam lingers on. Stratford depot still had a working steam breakdown crane until the late 1970s. Channelsea sidings contain an array of stock and a grounded GER coach body acting as a mess room. *(Author's Collection)*

Moving over 1000 tons of Freightliner wagons from a standing start off Channelsea curve was a challenge. The driver would need to gradually open the controller to full power, at the same time watching that the ammeter did not go into the red causing an overload. The position of the radiator shutters indicates that the loco is indeed under full power. Many of us will remember such sights. I often drove these trains in the early 1980s from Stratford to Willesden and return workings back to Stratford. Class 47 Co-Co 2750 H.P. No. 47010 (D1537) was withdrawn in December 1992 and cut up by Booth's in Rotherham one year later. *(Author's Collection)*

Some two years before the electrification to Norwich was completed, we see Class 86 (AL6) Bo-Bo electric loco No. 86007 (E3176/86407/86607) on a driver training trip, whilst changing crew at Stratford on 18th February 1985. The driver getting out of the cab is Stratford legend Peter Cross. Knowing Peter quite well, this sort of challenge, with new traction and new routes would have been right up his street. This loco carried the name "The Institution of Electrical Engineers" between 1987-1997 and is currently still in service with Freightliner. *Author's Collection)*

Thankfully, the current owner of 47579 "James Nightall G.C." has chosen the more traditional BR Blue livery for his preserved example instead of Network South East livery, which lasted from 1986 until 1994, seen here running through Stratford in April 1990. This loco entered service in 1964 as D1778, becoming 47183 in 1974 and finally 47579 in 1981. It was named as "James Nightall G.C." at March station on 28th September 1981 after one of the heroic war-time Soham disaster train crew. It also carried the names "St. Augustine" and "Christopher Wren" before being withdrawn in 2004. It is normally based at Mangapps Farm Railway Museum in Essex but is currently on loan to the Mid-Hants Railway. *(Author's Collection)*

On the 9th September 1962, just one week before the end of steam and one year after being officially withdrawn, this was the only surviving B12 (GER Holden S69) 4-6-0 No. 61572 at Stratford in store. Despite its external condition, it was returned to good working order and repainted for an outing on 5th October 1963 when it worked the "Wandering 1500" Railtour. This was an ambitious trip for such a veteran engine and eight coaches! The tour left Broad Street and visited Bedford, Northampton, Stratford-Upon-Avon and Rugby Midland, before a spirited run up the WCML back to Broad Street. It is now working on the North Norfolk Railway. *(Author's Collection)*

Looking rather well-kept is Class D16/3 4-4-0 No. 62548 in 1955 at Stratford. This is a Gresley 1930s rebuild from a GER S46 class, commonly known as a "Claud", after Lord Claud Hamilton, Chairman of the GER. This was a March (31B) engine at this time. Its career ended just two years later on 8th October 1957 and it was cut up at Stratford shortly afterwards. *(A.F. Grimmett Collection)*

Although the quality is poor, this is a rare colour view of a brand-new Class 114 Derby built 2-car DMU No. E56003 coupled to E50003 thought to be at the rear of the Engine Repair Shop at Stratford in the first week of November 1956. There is a record of this pairing working the Romford to Upminster branch on 12th November 1956, when only a week old and officially allocated to Lincoln (40A) depot. Note that Lincoln Central is shown in the destination indicator. The visit to the GE was very short lived, so it is very doubtful that Stratford would have fitted one of the local destination blinds. *(Author's Collection)*

(*left*) On a personal level, this image is one of the most poignant in the book. Having left school in April 1973, I applied for the position of a Traction Trainee (Secondman) at Stratford and walked through the doors behind Class 31 No. 31106 (D5524) into the inner sanctum of the Depot Manager's Offices. The entry exam was ridiculously simple (how else would I have got the job?) and by June I had started there as a raw recruit. This was a dream come true for a 16-year-old mad on trains, and I got paid for doing it. The sign over the office door survives in a private collection and 31106 is preserved at the Weardale Railway in County Durham. *(D. Sharp)*

(*bottom*) The year is 1961 and despite the electrification of the Enfield Town and Chingford line, all did not go to plan with the introduction of the new units. This meant that some of Stratford's many N7s had a brief stay of execution until the following year. Hoping to hear of another failed EMU are No's 69646 and 69697, which soldiered on until the bitter end of steam at Stratford in September 1962. The following twelve months must have been one of the darkest periods in the depot's history as literally hundreds of locos were cut up. *(Author's Collection)*

A superb line up inside Stratford's C shed in May 1976. All the regulars are here; Class 31 "Toffee Apple", Class 47 and Class 37. Stratford had an allocation of 121 locos at this time including 43 shunting engines. The red dots above the buffers on the 31 indicated electro-magnetic control between locos in multiple. The majority of 31s had the electro-pneumatic control, blue star code. Stratford's fitters were held in high regard by loco crews. It was rare to find NFF (No Fault Found) in the Repair Books! *(Author's Collection)*

Class 40 No. 40176 (D376) looks like it has the place to itself in August 1978, when its home shed was Healey Mills (Wakefield). It was always a pleasure to see a working 40 at Stratford and if you waited patiently, somebody would come along and fire it up. That sound was pure music to many of us. This nicely work-stained beast entered service in February 1962 at Camden (1B), spending its early days on express workings out of Euston. It was withdrawn in August 1981 and ironically, returned to Stratford, sadly only to be stored in the early months of 1982 before being cut up at Swindon Works in 1985. *(A.F. Grimmett Collection)*

Many of us will recall that the sight and sound of an English Electric Type 4 (Class 50) Co-Co 2700 H.P. working in the London area in the very early 1970s was extremely rare. I did once see one on Willesden depot in the early 70s, when it got through to Euston because of a failed electric loco at Crewe. Originally numbered from D400-D449, we had to travel all the way to Crewe to guarantee seeing them, as they ran double-headed from there to Glasgow before the electrification was completed. That all changed in 1974, when the wires to Glasgow were energised and the Class 50s were cascaded to the Western Region, becoming a common sight at Paddington. This is 50028 (D428) "Tiger" sitting at Stratford on 29th December 1978 after having worked to Temple Mills on a freight. *(B. Dann)*

The drivers' signing on point and mess room was just to the right of this image taken at Stratford on a bitterly cold 27th January 1979. A row of Class 31s is headed by 31106 and 31103 standing on No. 16 road. We would be serenaded by locos running all day long, as we sat in the mess room for up to eight hours on a spare turn. Far from being bored, there would be card games, a TV and a lot of good-humoured banter to while away the hours. There were several comedians amongst our ranks. The most legendary of all being Sid Woolnough. He once asked the foreman if he could hang some chains up in the mess room as it was approaching Christmas. The foreman said, "Of course you can Wooly". Sid went over to the breakdown crane and dragged about 30 feet of metal chain past the foreman's office. You can image the foreman's reaction! *(B. Dann)*

A long way from its home shed Gateshead (Newcastle), is BR built "Peak" 1Co-Co1 2700 H.P. Class 46 No. 46040 (D177) outside Stratford Diesel Repair Shops on a bitterly cold 26th January 1979. The reputation of the fitters here was second to none and despite there never being an allocation of Peaks at Stratford, they were occasional visitors to the depot having worked freight into Temple Mills. This example was a very early withdrawal; the end came the following year in December 1980. It was disposed of at Derby Works in April 1982. *(B. Dann)*

Newly named Class 47 No. 47169 (D1764/47581) "Great Eastern" is captured at Stratford on 4th March 1979. The actual naming ceremony was three days later at Liverpool Street. The nameplates were removed in August 1990 and withdrawal came in November 2000. The driver is Billy Hart, who is sadly no longer with us and standing by the steps is Barry Dann who has very kindly loaned many of his photographs for this volume. Barry is still driving (in 2018), so give him a wave as he speeds past on a Norwich to Liverpool Street service! *(B. Dann)*

Evidence of many months of hard work. Brake dust clings to the side of Class 47 Co-Co 2750 H.P. No. 47584 (D1775/47180) "County of Suffolk" in October 1982 outside the Diesel Repair Shops, Stratford. The loco was named at Ipswich station on 13th May 1979. The nameplates were removed by 1993. It was renamed "The Locomotive & Carriage Institution 1911" at Bristol Temple Meads in 1995. Withdrawal came in March 2000 and it was cut up at Booth's Rotherham in 2002. *(Author's Collection)*

Looking somewhat crestfallen, it is ironic that Class 40 No. 40003 (D203) should end up at Stratford during the latter months of 1982. Bodyside damage and no cab windows are signs of terminal illness. When built in 1958, Stratford (30A) was its first depot. It stayed until 1966, when it went to Ipswich (32B) and just a few months later it headed north where it would spend the rest of its days. It was withdrawn in September 1982 and after being stored at Stratford it was briefly used in Yorkshire for bridge testing, but doubtfully under its own power. Scrapping was carried out at Doncaster in January 1984. *(Author's Collection)*

The iconically named Class 40 "Lusitania" 40025 (D225) ended her days resting idly at Stratford between October 1982 and February 1983. Once part of the West Coast Main Line fleet, she was a long-time Manchester Longsight (9A) engine. The nameplates which once graced the bodyside have been removed several years hence, to be replaced by hand-painted examples. From Stratford, she was towed to Healey Mills (Wakefield), then met her fate at Doncaster in 1985. *(Author's Collection)*

The last of Stratford's Open Days was on 9th July 1983. A quiet moment before the hoards arrive is taken advantage of to capture new Class 58 Type 5 Co-Co 3300 H.P. No. 58002 outside B shed. This loco was new to Toton (Nottingham) depot on 24th May 1983. It was named "Daw Mill Colliery" in March 1988 and withdrawn in November 2000. *(Author's Collection)*

With his trademark beard and old BR driver's green jacket, my friend Keith Maeer poses in front of Cravens (Class 105) DMU on Stratford's fuel point, about to work one of the last Stratford to Tottenham Hale services on 5th July 1985. Lea Bridge station officially closed three days later but has gone through a remarkable transformation and after decades of neglect it reopened on 16th May 2016. Keith still has his beard and probably the jacket! *(K. Maeer)*

A very rare image of North British Loco Company Class 16 Bo-Bo 800 H.P. No. D8405 hauling a Loughton to Ramsgate excursion train over the London Underground Central line at South Woodford on 19th May 1962. This would have rejoined the BR system at Leyton, then Temple Mills East to Liverpool Street where the loco would either run round its train, or another 'trip cock' fitted locomotive would work the train over the East London line under the Thames to New Cross and the Kent coast. Did the NBL loco work all the way to Ramsgate? *(Author's Collection)*

An uncommon visitor to Temple Mills Yard is Class 56 Type 5 Co-Co 3250 H.P. No. 56089, one of the Doncaster built examples. Hauling a train of empty bogie bolsters, it is seen passing Manor Yard signal box. One overriding memory of this location was that every time we arrived here with a light engine, a shunter would appear from the mess room on the left and shout "Under Da Bridge", whereby he would disappear back into the mess room again; what a brilliant job! So, we would stand under Ruckholt Road bridge for what seemed like an eternity sometimes, breathing in copious quantities of diesel fumes before being called onto our train. *(Author's Collection)*

Pity that our photographer has accidentally chopped off the rear cab, but this is a rare colour view of Copper Mill Junction signal box between Lea Bridge and Tottenham Hale in 1964. Brush Type 2 A1A-A1A 1470 H.P. "Toffee Apple" No. D5512 dominates the scene taken from the south side of the line where the branch from Clapton Junction joins the start of the Lea Valley line. The signal box was taken out of use in February 1969 when its duties were transferred to Temple Mills West box. *(Author's Collection)*

(*above*) The next few images were captured by Doug Fairhurst circa 1968 just before the electrification of the Lea Valley line. They are mainly devoid of any 'traction', but not devoid of the atmosphere of a bygone age, captured and immortalised on film. Looking north at Northumberland Park, the faded green and cream paint left over from LNER days accompanied by BR dark blue enamels is perfection. A new footbridge has appeared raising the height required for overhead wires, but everything else is decades old, including the conveyor in the distance for Angel Road Gas Works. (*D. Fairhurst*)

(*right*) This nostalgic image is just as important as all the other paraphernalia that we have largely lost from today's railway. The humble BR Totem signs introduced shortly after Nationalisation in 1948 were a simple but hugely successful design, which we lived with for nearly 30 years. The signs themselves have become incredibly popular and collectable. The lovely dark blue examples here were the only totems on the whole BR network where the word 'Park' was abbreviated to just 'PK'. All the totem signs along the Lea Valley were removed during the electrification work, but fortunately the vast majority seem to have survived. (*D. Fairhurst*)

A delightful overall view of Northumberland Park in 1968 looking north. The two goods lines are still in use behind the Up Road platform. The station buildings would be replaced by the usual bus shelters. All the local passenger services were still DMU worked and there was a healthy amount of diesel worked freight. *(D. Fairhurst)*

The Gas Works at Ponders End provides an industrial backdrop contrasting with the tranquil stream in the foreground as a Class 125 DMU approaches the station with a Stratford to Cheshunt working in 1967. Ponders End South box was closed along with several others on the line in 1969. A Gas Works was established here in 1859 and one of the Company's first customers was the station master at Ponders End via a short pipe! *(D. Fairhurst)*

The early months of 1962 are tinged with sadness, as everybody with an interest in railways realises that these scenes are soon to disappear forever. A member of the loco crew took the opportunity to record this event, as one of the last surviving Stratford J15 0-6-0s, No. 65462 shunts a motley collection of brake vans into Ponders End Gas Works. Just a few months later in September, this loco and all its remaining brothers would be withdrawn from Stratford, but the story does not end there; No. 65462 was saved and became the only remaining example. It can be found working at the North Norfolk Railway, Sheringham. *(The late G. Wells)*

It was not thought necessary to electrify the Lea Valley line when the Bishops Stortford to Liverpool Street line via the reopened Southbury loop was modernised and reopened in 1960, even though the Lea Valley line, being almost dead straight, would have provided quicker journey times. So, for another nine years the trusty Class 125 DMUs would ply up and down, as seen here in October 1967, as a Cheshunt to Stratford 6-car set arrives at Ponders End in a mixture of green and blue liveries. *(D. Fairhurst)*

A sleepy Ponders End station looking north circa 1967 with just one passenger. Modernisation would soon see the old buildings reduced to rubble. The relatively new looking overbridge carried the A110; this had opened in 1963. In the distance is Brimsdown power station, which was still receiving coal by rail until 1971. *(D. Fairhurst)*

This historic old building at Ponders End on the Down side dated from the opening of the line by the Northern & Eastern Railway in 1840. Many decades of neglect and a lack of maintenance deemed it unsafe and it was demolished shortly after this view was taken. *(D. Fairhurst)*

An unusual view of a departing Class 125 Lea Valley line DMU heading towards Stratford in October 1967. The signal box can just be made out behind the footbridge and the Gas Works, which was in operation until 1971, dominates the background. *(D. Fairhurst)*

Traction would be a distraction! This is pure nostalgia, as the former South Street level crossing at Ponders End provides a few extra car parking spaces for commuters in 1967. The signal box just to the right closed in January 1969 and was demolished shortly afterwards. The classic cars were an everyday sight; have any of them survived? The level crossing closed after the new A110 bridge just north of the station opened in 1963. *(D. Fairhurst)*

Proof that the NBL Type 1 800 H.P. Class 16s really did perform some productive work! Much has been written about the failings of this small class, but they did venture out from Stratford depot, but rarely far, as fitters from other depots would have little knowledge of them. D8406 works an overhead line installation train at Brimsdown in 1968 while another classmate can be faintly seen in the distance. *(D. Fairhurst)*

The dying days of regular DMU operation on the Lea Valley line are captured on 26th November 1968, as a Class 125 3-car Derby set heads north at Brimsdown. The full electric service started on 9th March 1969, but much of the character of the stations had disappeared forever; they looked spartan and austere after being modernised. *(D. Fairhurst)*

The appearance of a Cravens 105 DMU on the Lea Valley anywhere north of Tottenham Hale was rather unusual in the 1970s. On this occasion the line north of Brimsdown was closed for weekend engineering work on the overhead lines in July 1977. The unit is No. E50360 and E 56420 from Stratford depot providing a shuttle service as far as the engineer's possession. The house in the background was the old station masters house. For many years it was occupied by Stratford driver Billy Knight and his family.

Bill found thousands of pre-grouping used wagon labels in the loft, which explains why many seen by collectors today have Brimsdown as the destination. *(Author's Collection)*

Doug's trusty camera captures the past in a way that very few photographers have. Maybe we become more sentimental with the passing of time, or is it just a sense of loss? Enfield Lock level crossing needs little explanation, but this scene was soon to change forever, as the footbridges would be demolished in favour of overhead electric supply. The 'traction' is a Ford Prefect 100E; over 100,000 of these were built between 1953 and 1959. *(D. Fairhurst)*

A Class 125 Derby built 3-car set leaves Waltham Cross & Abbey with a Stratford to Cheshunt service in 1967. A substantial goods yard was situated just north of the station on both sides of the line. This was sacrificed to speed up passenger services and it officially closed in 1969, but the connections to it had already been severed in this view, leaving just a trailing crossover between the main lines. *(D. Fairhurst)*

Rarer than the proverbial from a rocking horse! Hardly anybody bothered to capture the dying days of freight on the Beckton Gas Works branch, let alone in glorious colour, so this is a treat to find not one but two images. Brush Type 2 "Toffee Apple" No. D5512 (31012) passes over Manor Way level crossing on 7th August 1965 with a train of coke from the By-Product Works at Beckton for Temple Mills. The prefab houses and wonderful selection of road vehicles supplement a perfect scene. In the background can be seen the Northern Outfall Sewer being carried on an overbridge. *(Author's Collection)*

The same train has just passed over the level crossing on its journey from Beckton to Temple Mills. The derelict Manor Way signal box had been closed several years previously, but it was still used by the guard/shunter on the train to operate the wheel which closed the gates across the road. There really are no windows in the box; delightful. Once the train was clear of the crossing, the guard/shunter would open the gates for road traffic and get back in his brake van. Freight over this line ended on 1st June 1970. *(Author's Collection)*

N7 0-6-2T No. 69640 departs from North Woolwich in 1960 with a Palace Gates service. The thriving King George V Dock forms a wonderful backdrop and reminds us of a thriving port, all now gone forever. The docks may survive, but the character has changed beyond recognition today. This loco worked right up until the fateful end of steam at Stratford on 16th September 1962 and was cut up on site. *(Unknown/Author's Collection)*

A rather damp 6th October 1980 sees a Cravens Class 105 arriving at North Woolwich with a service from Camden Road. The driver is Stratford based John White, who like many drivers from this generation, is now enjoying his retirement. The section of line between Silvertown and North Woolwich has been closed since 2006. Crossrail has resurrected the line from Connaught Tunnel, through Silvertown station and towards North Woolwich, but the line now deviates and descends under the Thames via a new tunnel to Plumstead. *(Author's Collection)*

The same day in October 1980 at North Woolwich looking towards the GER 1854 station building which has Listed Status. From 1984 until 2008 a very fine railway museum was set up inside with the assistance of the local council, Passmore Edwards Museum and the Great Eastern Railway Society. Since the closure of the line in 2006, the front of the station has been kept in a reasonable state of repair, but the platform side has gradually been taken over by Mother Nature. *(Author's Collection)*

The period between 1985 and 1989 saw Southern Region 2EPB units running on the North Woolwich branch which was electrified on the 3rd rail system, enabling through running to Richmond. This is unit No. 6323 waiting to depart with a Richmond service in November 1985. The museum opened a year earlier and the unique GER Coffee Pot loco No. 229 stood on the old turntable site for several years. It is now being restored at a private railway workshop in the Dean Forest. *(Author's Collection)*

Suburban services in and out of Liverpool Street were dominated by the reliable AM6 (Class 306) EMUs until the introduction of Class 315s in late 1979. Most of us would have travelled on these in our youth and they still conjure up images of nostalgia and comfort that most modern trains seem to lack. The seat cushions were about a foot thick! On its last knockings at Ilford in 1979 is unit No. 018 being shunted from the Up platform to the Down side during overhead line work. There would have been a driver at each end for this manoeuvre, as changing ends on Ilford Flyover was frowned upon. *(Author's Collection)*

Taken the same weekend as the previous picture, a Class 105 Cravens set and a Derby built 3-car set work a Liverpool Street – Ilford shuttle as the overhead power was isolated from Manor Park to Liverpool Street. I'm certain that I was driving these units over this weekend. The back platform at Ilford is no more, due to platform extensions for Crossrail. *(Author's Collection)*

An early 1970s view of (AM6) Class 306 No. 032 fresh out of the paint shop at Ilford Car Sheds. Heavy maintenance and overhauls including traction motor replacements have been the backbone of keeping generations of EMUs on the road here. Many millions have been spent over the past few years to cater for the latest units including the Crossrail 345 fleet. *(Author's Collection)*

Looking uncharacteristically clean and tidy is Class 31 "Toffee Apple" No. 31019 in the sidings at Romford in 1977. This was one of two members of the class (the other being 31005) that were given this treatment including the white roof to work the "Toffee Apple Farewell Tour", which ran in October that year. Oddly, Paddington was chosen as the departure point and Bristol area branches were in the itinerary! A change in traffic requirements after the farewell tour meant that some of the Toffee Apples had a stay of execution for another 2/3 years. *(Unknown/Author's Collection)*

Romford once boasted substantial freight facilities, with the ability to handle upwards of a 100 wagons per day in the GER era. The Romford Brewery had its own railway system to the north of the station which ran under the main line in a tunnel to connect with the Lower Yard shown here. There were also sidings at the London end which were taken over by the Overhead Line Department. Another yard to the east was Victoria Road Coal depot. Once that closed in 1970 all the coal traffic was concentrated on the yard shown here on the south side of the station. This could only be reached by a perilous incline and this view, taken from the cab of a Class 31, shows a heavy load of 16T minerals being propelled gingerly down the incline in the early 1970s. A SR bogie brake van was kept in the yard specifically for this purpose. *(G. Weller)*

The Centenary of the opening of the Romford to Upminster branch line by the London Tilbury & Southend Railway took place on 5th June 1993. The preserved Class 306 unit No. 017 worked several shuttle trains over the branch all day and is seen here leaving Platform 1. The day was a great success and many stalls selling all sorts of goodies were located in the car park at Upminster. The branch is now part of the ever-growing Transport for London network. *(Author)*

If I start ranting about railway privatisation, it might fill another book! So, let's just look at another one of the varied liveries that have been thrust upon us over the years. This concoction is Class 37 No. 37379 in Mainline livery picking up wagons from the Overhead Line Depot at Romford in February 1997. It started life as D6926 new to Landore (Swansea) in 1964. It was renumbered 37226 in May 1974 and 37379 in July 1988. Nameplates carried here read 'Ipswich WRD Quality Assured'. These were applied in 1994, during the spell that it was allocated to Stratford (1993-1997). Withdrawal and scrapping came in 2007. *(A.F. Grimmett)*

Taken by yours truly on a sunny winter's day between Brentwood and Shenfield on the Down Main line whilst waiting at a red signal in the early 1980s. Class 37 No. 37166 (D6866) and another unidentified example would have had 3500 H.P. with the controller wide open and having no train behind is rather exciting! Between 1975 and 1984 this loco was allocated to Stratford apart from a brief spell at Immingham (40B) in 1981. This loco was new to Cardiff Canton (86A) in 1963 and its end came in 2010 with disposal at EMR Attercliffe the following year. *(Author)*

Most loaded oil trains from Thames Haven were worked by 37s and 47s during the 1980s, but empties being much lighter could be entrusted to a single Class 31 as seen here heading east at Barking on 11th April 1980 with No. 31148 (D5566/31448) in charge. This loco entered service at Stratford in November 1959 but was quickly relocated to Cambridge (31A). After many years it returned to Stratford in 1977. ETH was fitted and it became 31448 in 1984. The front gangway doors were a constant source of leaks and draughts. These have been removed and replaced by a sunken blanking plate giving the front end a strange appearance. *(Author's Collection)*

Originally built for outer suburban services out of Euston in the mid-1960s, most of the AM10 (Class 310) units came to the ER in 1988 and stayed until 2000. This is 310 095 approaching Barking from the Woodgrange Park direction with a diverted Liverpool Street to Shoeburyness service on 25th August 1994. From a driver's point of view, the brakes on some of these were often dreadful. They may well have been state of the art when built (they were the first EMUs with disc brakes), but by the time they arrived on the GE/LTS they had clocked up enormous mileages. I had the

misfortune of driving one up the Lea Valley one day, approaching Broxbourne I applied the brakes which failed to come on immediately. I ended up about a quarter of a mile beyond the station; none survive thankfully. *(Author's Collection)*

You certainly knew when one of these was imminent, as the ground literally shook with the colossal weight of 117 tons of locomotive and 100 tons of every loaded TEA tank wagon. Powering its way over Ripple Road level crossing on 10th October 1980 is Class 47 No. 47279 (D1981) heading west with an ex-Thames Haven working. This loco entered service in December 1965 at Gateshead and ended its days in December 2003, when it was cut up at Stockton-on-Tees. It was allocated to Stratford (hence the white roof) from May 1979 until January 1981 when it went to Tinsley. *(Author's Collection)*

Leaving the Ford's exchange sidings at Dagenham Dock is Class 47 No. 47016 (D1546), just before it was named "The Toleman Group" in May 1987. The nameplates were removed in October 1990. Between 1994-1998 it carried the name "Atlas". The internal railway at Ford's was vast in its heyday and during the late 1960s and 70s I witnessed several ex-BR Class 03 and Drewery Class 04s taking trains off into the abyss! Even today (2018), a much-truncated system survives, and Ford's have just four diesel locomotives. *(Author's Collection)*

Over the decades, there have been no less than 45 locomotives used at Ford's Dagenham plant when taking both steam and diesel into account. This is Peckett 0-6-0 Works No. 1890 Ford's No. 5 which was new to the plant in 1936 and still in use here in 1966. It was scrapped on site by the Romford Scrap and Salvage Co. in October 1969. This and the following two images were taken by ex-Stratford driver Gordon Wells, who sadly passed away in November 2018 aged 79 during the production of this volume, so it is a fitting tribute to a very knowledgeable and respected steam enthusiast. Gordon owned an industrial Manning Wardle steam loco "Newcastle", which is now at Beamish and a traction engine. *(G. Wells/A.F. Grimmett Collection)*

Originally ordered by Ford's in 1931, this is British Thompson Houston Bo-Bo 150 H.P. No. 1, still very much in use during 1966 at Dagenham. The design owed some of its heritage to the American 'Switcher' shunting locos used by the Ford company at their New Jersey plant in the US and three entered service at Dagenham. Shortly after this image was taken, this loco was preserved by the Kent & East Sussex Railway where it resides today, being the oldest working diesel electric shunter in the UK. The other two were sold/scrapped at the same time. *(G. Wells/A.F. Grimmett Collection)*

Peckett 0-6-0 No. 5 is seen again at Dagenham Dock with just some of the massive Ford plant visible. To the left is the London Tilbury Southend main line which runs through the middle of the Ford complex and heads towards Tilbury. Some of the Ford pallet vans with the company logo and blue livery can be seen parked up; these were used on the Halewood service. In the centre are thousands of tons of ingots destined for the foundry. *(G. Wells/A.F. Grimmett Collection)*

A truncated internal railway still exists at the Ford plant. This view, taken with permission, shows some of the sidings that pass under the A13 flyover, which would be a good vantage point were it not for the lorries thundering past. The loco is English Electric Vulcan Works No. D1124, an 0-4-0, which was new to Fisons Ltd at Avonmouth. It had other owners in private industry before arriving at Dagenham in 1993 and renumbered Ford's No. 1, replacing ex-BR Drewery 0-6-0 No. D2267, which was originally Ford's No.1. D2267 was then preserved at the North Norfolk Railway, but it was cut up circa 2003. The blue wagons are Arbel articulated covered car carriers. *(A.F. Grimmett)*

GREAT EASTERN SUBURBAN (CONTINUED)

A reminder that Baby Sulzers (Class 24s) were once a common sight at Stratford. When the first batch was built between 1958 and 1960, No's D5020-D5095 (24020-24095) were all allocated to either March (31B) or Ipswich (32B); some 75 locos! Here we see No's D5031/D5039/D5043 and D5053 lined up alongside one of the many steam sheds on 10th April 1960. *(Author's Collection)*

The brief period from early 1958 until September 1962 when both steam and diesel worked alongside each other in the East End was undoubtedly the most interesting time in Stratford's illustrious history. Seen here is J69/1 "Buckjumper" 0-6-0T No. 68609 alongside its Nemesis in the shape of Brush Type 2 A1A-A1A 1470 H.P. No. D5540 (built July 1959), which was already two years old when this image was captured in 1961. The Brush is outside the Jubilee shed, whilst its cohorts, Classes 15 (BTH) and 16 (NBL) are outside the relatively new B & C diesel shed. *(Author's Collection)*

LNER Y1/1 Sentinel Steam loco Departmental No. 39 (68131) stands at Stratford waiting to be scrapped in April 1963. This was last used for shunting at Chesterton Junction Sleeper Depot just north of Cambridge. It was moved from there to Stratford in October 1962 and spent several months languishing before being cut up. This was small fry compared to the hundreds of bigger locos being torched. Built in the mid-1920s, the LNER owned 24 of these tiny locos for shunting in smaller yards. *(R. Hummerston)*

The winter of 1962/3 was recorded as being one of the coldest ever recorded in the UK. It is not known if the weather was a factor in this collision between Brush Type 2 "Toffee Apple" No. D5509 and BTH Type 1 No. D8211 on Stratford shed during those bitterly cold months. The engines became lock buffered but there does not appear to be any other major damage and they would have probably returned to traffic quickly. *(The late G. Wells/A.F. Grimmett Collection)*

The year of 1958 was full of optimism when it came to diesel locomotive construction and the variety seemed overwhelming. The Brush factory at Loughborough is one of the most famous and successful builders. They constructed this delightful little diesel electric shunter (Works No. 100), No. D2999 in 1958 as a demonstration loco, hoping that more orders would follow. BR purchased it in September 1960 and Stratford became its home for seven years; seen here outside the New Shed in September 1963. It was used in several East End goods yards where tight curves existed. The power source was a Petter-Mclaren 200 H.P. engine connected to a single traction motor. Withdrawal came in October 1967, but it survived for another three years out of use until 1970 when it was cut up by Booth's of Rotherham. *(A.F. Grimmett Collection)*

Imagine the delight of visiting Stratford Depot in 1969 and finding at least seven (possibly more out of view) Class 20s at the back of the Diesel Repair Shop. This was Mecca for enthusiasts from all over the country and guided tours would often be organised. The locos carry a variety of liveries and would have still been Stratford allocated. By 1971 only three were allocated to Stratford; D8030, D8055 and D8056. *(Author's Collection)*

For a very brief period in June 1974 Class 45 1Co-Co1 2700 H.P. "Peak" No. 45006 (D89) "Honourable Artillery Company" was trialled on the Liverpool Street to Norwich service. It was loaned by Holbeck (55A) depot in Leeds, who were reluctant to let any of their allocation of Peaks go to the GE in large numbers, so they sent the poorest performing example on their books! The loco lost time on services in both directions, so the idea to have Peaks on the Norwich's was quickly dropped. During its short stay, No. 45006 was captured by an ex-Stratford man alongside Stratford's DMU shed. This loco was named in a regimental ceremony at Broad Street station on 9th June 1965 as the Regimental Headquarters was located nearby. It was withdrawn in September 1986 and cut up in 1988 by V. Berry in Leicester. *(C.K. Osta)*

The very first Stratford Open Day in 1979 (seen here) was such a great success that two more followed in 1981 and 1983. The freedom to roam around the depot and Diesel Repair Shops was hugely popular; can you see yourself amongst the crowd? Class 40 No. 40176 (D376) was very much still in service at this time. It was withdrawn two years later and returned to Stratford during 1982 for component removal before going to Swindon for cutting up. The Class 56 3250 H.P. Co-Co is one of the early Romanian built examples, No's 56001-56030, first introduced in 1976. *(A. Nugent)*

One of only a small class of just 25 locos built by the GER as D81s, they were reclassified J20s by the LNER. This was the most powerful of the GER freight engines. This is No. 64698 passing High Meads signal box between Channelsea Junction and Temple Mills on 18th March 1961. The load is redundant track panels from Leyton engineer's depot and has gone 'round the houses' (via Stratford) before heading to Chesterton Junction Sleeper Depot north of Cambridge. This is a reminder of the wholesale railway closures in East Anglia at this time; not forgetting the closure of virtually the whole Midland & Great Northern system in 1959. *(Author's Collection)*

Temple Mills Marshalling Yard underwent massive redevelopment in the late 1950s, which removed the old complex system of having eight different yards and a huge number of trip workings between them. The opportunity was also taken to divert the main line from the middle of the yard to the west side of the new yard as seen here in this 1958 view. About to pass under Ruckholt Road bridge with a freight from the Midland Region, is LMS 3F 0-6-0T "Jinty" No. 47241 of Kentish Town (14B) shed. The train is heading towards Stratford. *(Author's Collection)*

Between 1968 and 1970, there was a Freightliner service from London (Stratford) to Paris via the Dover to Dunkirk ferry. This is a very spruced up Brush Type 4 Co-Co 1750 H.P. No. D1758 (47164/571) about to depart from the Freightliner Terminal at High Meads with the inaugural service on 22nd April 1968. Stratford's legendary painters have even painted the loco tyres white for the occasion. The Stratford driver posing for the cameraman is Peter Wagstaff. This was long before the Channel Tunnel, the European Union and the Brexit fiasco. If only we could turn the clock back. (*The late G. Saville Collection*)

Taken from the rear of a North Woolwich to Stratford Low Level DMU in the mid-1960s, we are looking towards Thames Wharf Junction signal box in the distance as we approach Canning Town station. The lines on the rising 1 in 30 gradient to the right, continued around Bow Creek and Pepper Warehouse sidings, which closed on 1st July 1968. *(Author's Collection)*

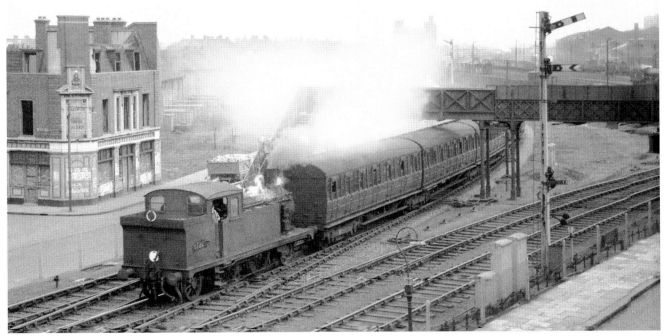

One of Stratford's 2-4-2T F5s No. 67211 passes the site of Tidal Basin station as it rounds the curve near Thames Wharf Junction in 1957, just prior to the class being replaced by N7s on the North Woolwich to Palace Gates service. Tidal Basin station closed on 15th August 1943 after bomb damage had caused considerable damage in 1941. The tracks to the right served the large PLA Victoria Dock exchange sidings which covered a large expanse of land all the way to Custom House in the distance. *(B. Pask)*

(*left*) Having just left the PLA exchange sidings at the PLA Victoria Dock, Baby Sulzer (Class 24) Type 2 Bo-Bo 1160 H.P. No. D5066 waits for the signal with Victoria Dock Road in the background. All freight from this yard ended on 1st May 1970 when the PLA suddenly stopped all rail traffic from Victoria Dock almost overnight. This loco was allocated to Finsbury Park (34G) in 1964 when this picture was taken. As 24066 this loco was withdrawn in December 1976 and cut up a year later. (*Author's Collection*)

(*bottom*) The 15.51 North Woolwich to Tottenham Hale service formed of a Class 104 Birmingham Railway Carriage & Wagon built 1958 DMU leaves Silvertown, which retains much of its unrestored charm of bygone days, on 6th June 1973. The former Up Road platform had closed to passengers on 24th August 1969 and the signal box, the base of which is still in situ, closed at the same time. The section from Custom House to North Woolwich was effectively two single lines from this date (controlled from Custom House); one (former Down Road) for passenger and the other (former Up Road) for freight. (*R. Hummerston*)

Silvertown yard still had a healthy delivery of wagons every day in the early 1970s, but just one business on Factory Road towards North Woolwich was still rail connected. This is Silvertown yard pilot Class 08 0-6-0 350 H.P. No. D3532 (08417) making a delivery to Standard Telephone and Cables Ltd. premises on 6th June 1973. North Woolwich station is behind the photographer. *(R. Hummerston)*

A cracking view of LNER Thompson designed B1 4-6-0 No. 61329 storming past Ilford Flyover with a Down Road express from Liverpool Street in June 1959. This was a Stratford (30A) allocated engine. Upon the end of steam on the GE in September 1962 it was transferred to Doncaster (36A) until being withdrawn and cut up by Cohen's of Kettering in 1966. The second compartment in the leading carriage has a driver's tea can on the ledge, indicating that a crew were travelling 'passenger on the cushions' to either their home depot or to take up another working. *(Author's Collection)*

The same location a few years later sees Brush Type 2 A1A-A1A 1470 H.P. No. D5637 (31213) with a short Up Road fully fitted freight for Temple Mills. The guard would be riding in the back cab to keep an eye on the train. This loco was new to Stratford in July 1960. It was fitted with ETH equipment and renumbered 31465 in March 1985. It survives at Barrow Hill depot. The footpath out of view on the left separated the local cemetery from the railway and was my favourite haunt as a kid; the railway not the cemetery! *(Author's Collection)*

The 92 AM6 (306) units were originally an LNER design and some early units had LNER axle box covers. The Second World War delayed their introduction and the electrification of the Liverpool Street to Shenfield line. This is the first 3-car unit 01 (306001), with driving car E 65201 leading, after delivery to Ilford Car Sheds in March 1949. Note that there is no unit number on the front; the numbers were initially carried on a circular disc on the lamp bracket. Trials between Ilford and Chadwell Heath ran from March until September, then the full service to Shenfield began in November 1949. *(Author's Collection)*

Originally built by the North Eastern Railway for the short-lived electrified Newport to Shildon railway to haul coal trains, this Bo-Bo 1100 H.P. electric loco saw further use as the Ilford Car Sheds depot shunting engine No. 26510 from 1949 until 1960. One of ten built between 1914-1919, it became redundant on Teesside due to the 1930s recession and entered Doncaster works in 1941 for conversion to a banking loco for the Woodhead route, but this idea was later abandoned. It languished at Doncaster until 1947, then went to store at South Gosforth car sheds until its arrival at Ilford in 1949, where it gained the nickname 'Dennis'. It was cut up at Doncaster in 1964. *(T. Wright)*

One of the first AM7/Class 307 units on display at Ilford Car Sheds in 1956. There were 32 built at BR Eastleigh for the Southend Victoria service. As built, they were for D.C. use only, but larger numbers of EMUs coming into use put more and more strain on the current supply, so 6.25kv and 25kv A.C. conversions were carried out at Eastleigh in 1960. This is unit No. 05s, which was rebuilt as unit No. 105. The class was refurbished in the early 1980s, with open seating areas. They served Essex commuters well until the arrival of the 321s between 1988 and 1991. *(Author's Collection)*

The electrification of the Shenfield to Southend route in the late 1950s and the introduction of new AM7 (307) units, prompted the addition of the New Shed at the eastern end of Ilford Car Sheds to maintain and clean the new stock. The shed was constructed on the site of the former Newbury Park triangle which closed in 1956. This is the view inside the new building shortly after the official opening in 1958. *(Author's Collection)*

Undoubtedly a triumph of EMU design, the AM9/309 Clacton stock were a product of the Wilkes & Ashmore Company of designers, who had previously worked on the AM3/303 Glasgow Blue Trains with their distinctive wrap round windscreens and the AM5/305 units for the North East London Chingford and Enfield services. The corridor connections were an essential part of the design due to the length of journey time between London, Clacton and Walton, but the appearance would have been even more sleek without them. This is a brand new 4-car set No. 622 at Ilford Car Sheds Ley Street end in 1962. *(Author's Collection)*

The Class 90 Bo-Bo 5000 H.P. electric locomotives were introduced between 1987 and 1990 on the WCML. A fleet of 50 were built and the majority are still in service. Greater Anglia took delivery of 90001-90015 in 2004 to replace the Class 86 locos on the Norwich service. At the time of writing (2018), even the Class 90s have a very short lifespan left on the Norwich service as they are due to be replaced in 2019/20 by Class 745 Stadler EMUs. This undated view shows No. 90028 on what is possibly a test train or driver training trip of coal hoppers passing Ilford Car Sheds in Inter-City livery. (Author's Collection)

A rare early view of a brand-new pair of AM6 (306) 3-car units at Chadwell Heath working a test train from Ilford Car Sheds in 1949. The line was initially only energised as far as Chadwell Heath on 23rd March 1949. The driver is changing ends and an important looking gentleman in a trilby hat is keeping an eye on the proceedings. Note the tail lamp on the back of the unit. Beyond the unit, looking towards Goodmayes, can be seen the original GER Chadwell Heath signal box, which had just been made redundant buy the new colour light signalling system coinciding with the new overhead supply. The electric service to Shenfield started on 26th September 1949. *(A.F. Grimmett Collection)*

Class AM8/1 (308/1) unit No. 135 approaches Romford in 1966 with empty stock from Ilford Car Sheds in what is believed to be an official BR view to show off the newly applied BR blue paint scheme. It is a pity that the cheapskates at Head Office did not use colour film! Only an official photographer would have been allowed to stand so close to the main line. A Class AM9 (309) Clacton set has only just passed by in the London direction. *(Author's Collection)*

The push to eradicate steam from many inner suburban branch lines was well underway by 1956, with the Romford-Upminster-Grays and Wickford-Southminster lines being early candidates for new DMUs to take over. This view of a Derby built 3-car set at Romford was taken circa 1959. The LT&SR opened the branch in 1893 and before the connecting footbridge over South Street was built, passengers had to leave the LT&SR station, cross South Street and enter the GER station by a separate entrance due to competition between the two companies. The footbridge was not installed until 1934. The branch was electrified in 1986. *(Author's Collection)*

By any standards, the "Liverpool Street Leapfrog" railtour on 29th February 1992 was a mammoth undertaking for the organisers and the railway operators. Organised by 538 Railtours, it covered a huge area of the GE suburban and LT&SR network. It started from Waterloo at 07.30 and did not get back there until 21.45. Space precludes the full itinerary, but in a nutshell, Liverpool Street, Enfield Town, South Tottenham, Shoeburyness, Tilbury Riverside, Fenchurch Street, Gas Factory Junc, Bow Junc, Southend Victoria, Temple Mills, Hertford East, Liv St, North London line, Willesden Junc and Kew were visited! Class 33 No. 33116 (D 6535) and 4TC sets 410/417 worked the whole tour, which is seen passing Romford on the Up Main around 16.30. Quite a marathon. The Chingford branch should have been visited, but this was cancelled due to late running. *(A.F. Grimmett Collection)*

Believe it or not, this very clean looking J15 0-6-0 No. 65465 captured in a siding at Gidea Park in the late 1950s is very much in steam and not abandoned as it might appear. Allocated to Colchester (30E) it has worked a freight into the yard which occupied the site of the former Provender Store which had previously burnt down. In the background is Gidea Park signal box, which stood until 1997. *(North Norfolk Railway Collection)*

We boldly go to Shenfield, a far-off outpost of East End Traction! Due to the electrification of the Manchester, Sheffield and Wath lines via Woodhead tunnel being unfinished in late 1950, the new Gorton built locomotives destined for the route were tested on the Great Eastern which had the same 1500 volt D.C. overhead traction supply system. EM1 (Class 76) Bo-Bo No. (E)26002 stands at Shenfield during a trial run with a train of empty coal wagons on Sunday 12th November 1950. The first 10 locos underwent trials on the GE for seven months until June 1951. Only one example of the 58 locos built has been preserved. No. E26020 (76020) is part of the National Collection. *(C.J. Marsden Collection)*

Preserved steam certainly still runs on the main line, but East Anglia is not so well served as other parts of the country. This scene will certainly never be repeated due to the only surviving B12 4-6-0 No. 61572 not being main line certified. This is No. 61535 of Ipswich (32B) shed approaching Shenfield with a London bound stopping service in 1952. The B12s (GER S69 Holden design) were a common sight throughout East London and Essex, particularly on the Southend Victoria line prior to electrification in 1956, but all 81 were withdrawn by 1961. (*Unknown/Author's Collection*)

The electrification of the Shenfield to Southend Victoria line was completed in 1956 with the official opening using electric rolling stock taking place on 31st December that year. This is one of the earliest services in the first month of 1957 at Shenfield with brand new AM7 (Class 307) 4-car EMUs. As built, they had four-position white light indicators with the tail light in the middle of the cluster. The 06s numbering was later replaced by 106; the 's' indicating Southend stock. *(Author's Collection)*

Possibly in connection with electrification work on the Colchester and Clacton lines during 1959, we witness the appearance of an early Cravens (Class 105) DMU in platform 4 at Shenfield on 22nd February. The destination of Brightlingsea is another reminder of the Beeching branch line cuts of the 1960s; this one branching off from the Clacton line at Wivenhoe, closed in June 1964. Introduced in 1956, there were eventually 302 Cravens cars built. Only three survive in preservation due to the problem of asbestos in their original construction. Those of us driving these were blissfully unaware of the hidden dangers lurking behind the inner walls. The same applied to many other DMU and EMU types. *(Author's Collection)*

English Electric Type 3 Co-Co 1750 H.P. No. D6708 (37008) pauses at Shenfield & Hutton Junction in 1961 with an Up Road express. New to Ipswich (32B) in February 1961, it moved to Stratford just four months later. The connection to the former goods yard has been severed from the Down Main line. This area was later turned into a car park. The signal box closed in May 1981 and was demolished shortly afterwards. (Author's Collection)

LONDON TILBURY & SOUTHEND LINE

LMS Stanier 4-6-2T 4P 3-cylinder No. 42502 passes over the North London Railway Poplar line near Campbell Road Junction on its way from Fenchurch Street to Shoeburyness in 1959. To the right we can faintly see the NLR route and Devons Road shed is out of view on the right. This is the point where the Underground District line joins the LT&SR line. Designed for use on the LT&SR in 1934, there were 37 3-cylinder locos in this class and only No. 42500 survives as part of the National Collection. *(F. Church)*

Captured coming off the North London curve between Campbell Road Junction and Bromley-by-Bow station is English Electric Type 1 Bo-Bo 1000 H.P. No. D8016 (20016) in July 1959. This curve, which ran behind Bow Works, closed shortly after this view was taken. It was used by passenger trains at various points in time, but these had ceased by 1935. The train of tanks would be destined for Thames Haven, and the loco carries one of the distinctive 'target' numbers which were seen on virtually all workings from Devons Road (1D) shed, where this engine was allocated from 4th January 1958 until the depot closed in 1964. It was then transferred to Stratford. *(Author's Collection)*

Between 13th December 1954 and 5th February 1955, the unique prototype LMS Ivatt designed diesel-electric Bo-Bo 827 H.P. No. 10800 in black livery was tested extensively over the LT&SR lines. It is seen here heading towards London on a test train, having just passed through East Ham station. It was tested on freight, shunting and passenger workings. By very good fortune, I have a copy of the official report from 1955, which is fascinating reading and worthy of an article in the future perhaps. It covered hundreds of miles and visited every corner of the LT&SR system including Thames Haven, but was rarely photographed. The trials showed that this loco was underpowered for express passenger working, but many lessons were learnt, providing valuable information for the next generation of diesels, particularly the Class 15 and 16 Bo-Bo 800 H.P. locos. *(Author's Collection)*

Heading west approaching East Ham, this is Brush Type 2 "Toffee Apple" No. D5511 (31011) on 31st January 1959 with a freight. The destination is unrecorded, but it could have been one of the goods depots still in operation on the approaches to Fenchurch Street, as Haydons Square, East Smithfield and Commercial Road goods depots were still in operation in 1959. The curve to the left connected East Ham to Woodgrange Park, which closed to all traffic in November 1959. The site is now occupied by a housing estate. *(Author's Collection)*

Certainly not a common sight on the London Tilbury & Southend lines; a Thompson B1 4-6-0 No, 61361 waits at the foot of the newly opened Barking Flyover in late 1959. This was a Southend Victoria (30D) allocated engine in the mid-1950s, but the letter on the shedplate is unreadable. The engine is most likely on its way to Ripple Lane to work a freight. To the left is Howards chemical factory and the waste ground is where I spent many long hours in the early 70s trainspotting. Nothing this rewarding was seen unfortunately, as steam had long been banished from East Anglia. *(Author's Collection)*

Construction of the Barking Flyover and rebuilding of the station took over three years to complete, with the official opening of the station by Her Majesty The Queen taking place on 15th February 1962. This view from the almost finished flyover was taken on 29th March 1959 as Brush Type 2 "Toffee Apple" D5501 (31001) propels an engineer's scrap train towards the station. Note that the signals are 'off' for the movement and the crew are in the other end of the loco. *(Author's Collection)*

In 1959 this was considered to be the most modern traction and infrastructure in the country! A new locomotive, just nine months old and a new flyover at Barking to alleviate decades of delays caused by the junctions at both ends of the station. Toffee Apple Brush Type 2 No. D5518 descends towards the station with a train of LMS stock from the Woodgrange Park line on 20th July 1959. *(A.F. Grimmett Collection)*

After a serious collision on Stratford depot in 1967 with a Class 15 BTH, Brush Type 2 No. D5518 was so badly damaged that both cabs had to be cut off. A decision was made to rebuild the loco but with standard headcode box fitted cabs and blue star standard coupling equipment. It therefore ceased to be a Toffee Apple and carried on into preservation as 31101. This previously unpublished view shows it inside the DRS at Stratford shortly after the collision. *C. Blackwell)*

Shortly after the opening of the Barking Flyover, we witness North British Locomotive Company (Class 21) Type 2 Bo-Bo 1100 H.P. No. D6112 coming off the flyover with a train of empty stock comprising of LMS vehicles on 22nd August 1959. This locomotive appears to have had a troublesome life. It was sent to Scotland in 1960 along with its classmates and spent more time in storage than it did in service! It was cut up in 1972 and none survive. Whilst there are clearly a few overhead electrification masts starting to appear, it would be over two years before the LT&SR OHL system went live in November 1961. *(A.F. Grimmett Collection)*

Occasionally, an old black and white negative will reappear from the past and be dismissed by many people as being insignificant. This negative took over an hour's work in Photoshop, as it had many hundreds of tiny white dots. This image obviously has no traction, but is more than worthy of inclusion, as it captures the old Barking station looking east just before the massive rebuilding in the late 1950s. The decades of soot and grime are about to be banished forever, to be replaced by modern steel and concrete. The old BR dark blue enamel Totem signs would be hugely collectable today, as none are known to survive due to the rebuilding, where they seem to have all been scrapped. *(Author's Collection)*

Brush Type 2 No. D5536 (31118) passes through Barking with a Southend Central bound excursion in the summer of 1959. This loco entered service in June 1959, so would be just a few months old. The new flyover is open for traffic, but the station redevelopment has only just begun. The old Barking West signal box can be seen faintly. In Platform 5, a steam hauled service for Fenchurch Street can just be made out. *(Unknown/Author's Collection)*

To cope with the additional traffic to and from Ripple Lane Marshalling Yard, the section of line between Barking and Ripple Lane was widened from two tracks to four as part of the 1955 Modernisation Scheme. The work was spread over several years in the late 1950s. This is the new Ripple Road signal box which replaced the former LT&SR Rippleside box on 14th September 1961 looking west. *(Author's Collection)*

Costing many millions, the marshalling yard and locomotive depot at Ripple Lane came into use in 1959/60 to much fanfare. Early residents here on 31st April 1960 are three Brush Type 2 "Toffee Apple's" and two North British Type 2 (Class 21) Bo-Bo 1100 H.P. engines in the D6110-D6119 range. By August 1960 all the Stratford based NBL locos were sent to Scotland, in order that they would be closer to the NBL factory when they failed, which they did often! In the background can be seen the incline to the short-lived hump marshalling yard. Changing traffic patterns caused a drastic reduction in the need for hump shunting and the yard was levelled just a few years later. *(Author's Collection)*

Prior to 1964, the transport of new cars by BR was limited to flat wagons, both single and bogied vehicles. The introduction of the semi-fixed formation of 4-car Cartic wagons, built at Ashford made a huge difference to the industry and 30 cars could be moved by one 4-car set. This is the inaugural Dagenham Dock to Halewood (Liverpool) service on 7th July 1966 with Class 47 No. D1758 (47164/47571/47822 and rebuilt 57305) in charge for the Dagenham to Willesden section, where an AC Electric loco would take the train north. (Author's Collection)

A rare but poor view of the RCTS "East London Railtour No. 2" which ran on 24th March 1956. Starting at Fenchurch Street with BR Standard 2-6-4 Tank No. 80080 in charge, the tour is seen here at Upminster before running across to Romford, then on to Beckton, Millwall Junction and ending at Broad Street. The second leg of the tour was hauled by double-headed LMS 3F "Jinties" No's. 47351 and 47484. The full itinerary can be viewed on the Six Bells Junction website under The Railtour Files. In the background, minus its roof is Upminster loco shed. *(Unknown/Author's Collection)*

A superb view of a nearly new Class 114 Derby built 2-car DMU at Upminster on 31st March 1957. These units were more associated with Lincoln (40A) depot, but for the first few months of their early career they (E50029-E50034/E56029-E56034) were allocated to Stratford and were recorded as working on both the Romford to Upminster and Upminster to Grays branches. In 1957 there was still a junction across the Underground third rail lines, so it was possible to travel from Romford to Grays direct. This is unit number E56034 and E50034 in the Up side siding. *(A.F. Grimmett Collection)*

This is the pioneer Metropolitan-Cammell 'Lightweight' DMU comprising of two 2-car sets at Upminster circa 1959/60, as electrification masts are appearing. Although many hundreds would eventually be produced and become a common sight across East Anglia, the leading Driving Motor Brake Second is the first of the class E79047, built in 1955. It is working a Grays service via Ockendon. *(Author's Collection)*

Electrification of the LT&SR routes took many years and many millions of pounds, but the full electric service was only gradually introduced during 1961/2, with June 1962 being the month when steam was finally eliminated from passenger use. That said, excursion traffic from other regions would make occasional visits and some freights were steam worked until September 1962. This is the new order, unit No. 299 on 14th July 1961 at Upminster, although it has obviously been in use for several months, as the grease-caked buffers and grime testify. BR ordered 112 of these AM2/302 4-car sets for use on the Fenchurch Street, Tilbury and Shoeburyness services. They were built in two batches at York and Doncaster between 1958-1960. *(Author's Collection)*

This is Sunday 31st July 1960 and Stratford's Brush Type 2 "Toffee Apple" No. D5514 has been pressed into service due to the demand for extra trains on the LT&SR. The driver waits for 'right away' from the Westcliff platform staff with a Southend Central bound service. Steam was still in use at this time and whilst there is evidence of new overhead line structures, it would not be fully energised over the whole line until November 1961. *(A.F. Grimmett Collection)*

On the same day as the previous view, another "Toffee Apple" Brush Type 2 No. D5507 (31007) calls at Westcliff with a London bound service. This loco was new to Stratford in April 1958 and stayed there its entire life until it was withdrawn in November 1976. *(A.F. Grimmett Collection)*

NORTH EAST LONDON

Brush Type 2 No. D5664 (31237) passes through Hackney Downs on 22nd January 1962 with a Liverpool Street to Cambridge express. This loco was new to March (31B) depot in November 1960 and ended its days in July 1995. It was not cut up until September 2004 at Stockton-on-Tees. On the extreme left is the corner of the modern Hackney Downs signal box which replaced the old GER mechanical box on 29th May 1960. *(Book Law Publications)*

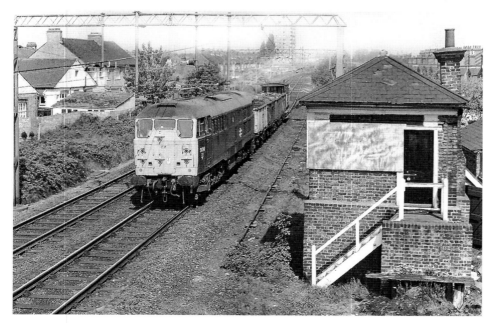

A very rarely photographed freight in the 1970s was the Temple Mills to White Hart Lane goods, seen here passing the former Edmonton Junction signal box on 7th May 1976. The sidings at White Hart Lane were only accessible from the Up Side, so the train ran down the Lea Valley to Cheshunt, sometimes dropping wagons off, before heading up the Southbury Loop line and onto White Hart Lane. The empties would travel back to Temple Mills via the Seven Sisters to South Tottenham curve. White Hart Lane goods yard closed on 2nd July 1977. *(R. Hummerston)*

A fascinating busy scene at Northumberland Park on the Lea Valley line in 1955 looking north. In the foreground is an unidentified D16 "Claud" 4-4-0 standing by the water tower and ash pit. An almost new Drewery diesel shunter lurks on the reception road, whilst an N7 0-6-2T passes with a northbound Hertford East service. In the distance Northumberland Park station can be faintly seen and beyond that is Angel Road Gas Works. This whole area is now occupied by the London Underground Victoria Line depot. (Author's Collection)

(*left*) An unidentified LNER Gresley designed 2-6-0 K3 storms through Northumberland Park in 1959 with a northbound freight. The freight lines are far left. Commuters on the Lea Valley, Cambridge and Stansted Airport have been begging for decades to have four tracks reinstated on this very busy route. A third track has been laid from Lea Bridge to the new station at Meridian Water, replacing Angel Road, but access to it from the north is not currently possible. *(B. Pask)*

(*bottom*) Commuters at Brimsdown are disturbed by the passing of B17/6 4-6-0 Football class No. 61655 "Middlesbrough" as it charges through the station with a southbound Cambridge to Liverpool Street service in 1957. Just two years later this loco was withdrawn from Cambridge (31A) shed and cut up at Doncaster. Tragically, the whole class of 73 locomotives was wiped out by September 1960. *(B. Pask)*

In the 1950s Hertford East (30B) shed only had an allocation of about a dozen steam locos, mainly N7 0-6-2Ts. This is a visitor in the shape of Stratford based J15 0-6-0 No 65463 in the mid-1950s. The small 2-road shed closed once the Hertford East branch was electrified in November 1960 and it was demolished the following year. This engine was withdrawn in November 1959 and cut up at Stratford Works; ironically, its birthplace. (Book Law Publications)

One of the pleasures in compiling these books, is the challenge of finding out where some images are taken. This original negative came along without any form of identification, but my gut instinct was a Lea Valley line station, which turned out to be Cheshunt in the 1930s. Two contributors carried out detective work, including the studying of a 1930s telephone directory to hunt down Cook & Co. Ltd behind the Up Road platform! The B12 4-6-0 No. 8511 (61511) in LNER Apple Green roars through with a Liverpool Street bound express. This loco was withdrawn in 1952. *(Author's Collection)*

Brush Type 2 No. D5695 is braking hard as it approaches Bishops Stortford in 1961 when just a few months old. This one had to be included as the loco is a personal favourite. In 1974 it became 31265 and was renumbered 31430 in 1983 when ETH was fitted. In this guise, it was named "Sister Dora" in 1988 and was purchased for preservation upon withdrawal. It spent several years at the Mid-Norfolk Railway before being purchased by Martin Staniforth who kept it for several years at Mangapps Farm Railway Museum in Essex where I had the privilege of helping with the restoration and occasional driving turns. It is currently at the Spa Valley Railway. *(M. Staniforth)*

The Railway Correspondence & Travel Society ran the "Great Eastern Suburban Railtour" on 12th November 1960 and two colour views of this engine J69/1 0-6-0T No. 68619 were used on the last page of London's East End Steam. I mentioned how the locomotive, normally used as the London Pilot, expired at Wood Street on its way to Chingford with low boiler pressure and had to be assisted by N7 No. 69687. Here is the errant ''Buckjumper'' at Wood Street waiting for the assisting N7 in the background which has just come off the soon to close Wood Street loco depot. *(Author's Collection)*

Quite clearly not the East End, but it certainly originated from Ford's at Dagenham. Pioneer Brush Type 2 A1A-A1A 1470 H.P. No. D5500 (31018) passes Hampstead Heath signal box on the North London line with the Dagenham to Halewood train in 1968. The "Toffee Apple" would come off at Willesden High Level (Stonebridge Park) sidings to be replaced by an LM electric loco for the journey to Liverpool. *(Author's Collection)*

A little-know DMU service provided for staff only ran over the London Underground Central Line to Epping and Loughton throughout the 1960s via a connection at Leyton station. This is a Stratford based Class 125 Derby 3-car Lea Valley line set approaching South Woodford station with the empty stock for Stratford depot after working the very last service, the 06.56 Liverpool Street to Loughton on 31st May 1970. *(R. Hummerston)*

This is another view which took several hours of research and, with the help of some friends, we deduced that British Thompson-Houston (Class 15) Type 1 Bo-Bo 800 H.P. No. D8201 is approaching South Hampstead station on the WCML with a freight bound for the North London line, which it would gain via Primrose Hill and Camden Road. The 3-headed colour light signal is believed to be a distant for the junction at the London end of Primrose Hill Tunnels, the entrance of which is just beyond the station behind the photographer. Another unpublished out of focus view taken at the same time, shows a third set of tracks to the right with third rail power supply. The destination is uncertain, but the Type 1 would have most likely taken the train of insulated containers over at Willesden. *(Author's Collection)*

I have chosen to end this tour with two of Arthur Nugent's legendary images from the early 1960s. Arthur was a fitter at Camden shed (1B) and had access to areas out of bounds to Joe Public! Leaving Camden Freight Depot with a northbound working in June 1962 is Britannia class 7P6F 4-6-2 No. 70017 "Arrow" producing copious quantities of steam from every angle and coal piled high for the journey ahead. In the background is Primrose Hill station which closed on 28th September 1992 and beyond that is the Grade II Listed London & Birmingham Railway Roundhouse built in 1846. It is used as a performing arts centre today. *(A. Nugent)*

Just across the main line lay Camden shed, which is hosting Baby Sulzer Bo-Bo 1160 H.P. (Class 24) No. D5146 (24146) in May 1962. This loco was first allocated to Willesden (1A) in December 1960 and spent the next few years there until April 1964 apart from a brief spell of crew training at Monument Lane (21E) in 1961. Alongside is the nose of English Electric Type 4 (Class 40) No. D301 (40101), which was new to Crewe (5A) in November 1960. Just one month later it was briefly allocated to Camden, but by the time of this view it was a Longsight (9A) engine and is carrying a 9A shedplate. With the increase in electric locos on the WCML, the shed closed in 1966. (A. Nugent)